DATE DUE

Demco, Inc. 38-293

THE
EUROPEAN QUESTION
AND THE
NATIONAL INTEREST

THE EUROPEAN QUESTION AND THE NATIONAL INTEREST

Jeremy Black

© The Social Affairs Unit 2006
All rights reserved

British Library Cataloguing in Publication Data
A catalogue record of this book is available from the British Library

All views expressed in this publication are those of the author, not those of the Social Affairs Unit, its Trustees, Advisers or Director

Book production by Crowley Esmonde Limited
Printed and bound in Belgium

ISBN 1-904863-08-6

Social Affairs Unit
314-322 Regent Street
London W1B 5SA
www.socialaffairsunit.org.uk

For Andrew Mitchell

CONTENTS

Preface		9
CHAPTER 1	Introduction: Turning Points and Contingencies	11
CHAPTER 2	Deep History: Britain and Europe, the Historical Background	26
CHAPTER 3	'Joining Europe': Britain and Europe, the Historical Background	43
CHAPTER 4	A Very Rocky Marriage	67
CHAPTER 5	New Labour and the Problem of National Identity	88
CHAPTER 6	Future Scenarios	117
CHAPTER 7	Conclusions: Crisis of a Political System?	143

PREFACE

This book aims to provide a historical context for the debate over Britain's relations with, and within, the European Union at a time when the latter is more than ordinarily in difficulties and the relationship therefore problematic. Whereas, in other countries, there is opposition to the terms of relationships within the European Union, in Britain there is not only this but also widespread hostility to, or at least, uneasiness about, the very relationship itself. Britain has also had a very ambiguous relationship with the idea of a European league. This indeed is an aspect of the very contrast between Britain and the Continent, a contrast, moreover, which is not limited to just one part of the political spectrum. Both major political parties were divided over joining the European Economic Community in 1973. The discussion is also located in terms of differing definitions of national interest, more specifically the confused Labour, or even more specifically, 'New Labour' response to the issue of how best to conceive a post-imperial identity for Britain. Some of the historical background may appear unnecessary to older readers, but it is surprising how little students know about the history of Britain's relations within Europe, and that has helped prompt this book.

Fellow academic historians will know that this is not the sort of book we should write. It does not count in Research Assessment Exercises, risks compromising our scholarly reputation, provides hostages to academic critics, and is regarded as the sort of thing best left to non-academics. I am, however, dissatisfied with this negative and overly cautious concept of the academic world. I feel that we ought to engage with topics of public interest, and that recent or contemporary times are not outside the scan of the historian. All too often, the academic seeks to offer Olympian detachment and oracular judgment based on the idea of definitive knowledge. This is inappropriate for the study of the past. Instead, the values of scepticism that best frame the attempt to understand historical processes are also appropriate to consideration of present and future developments.

It is a great pleasure to thank Michael Mosbacher for inviting me to write this book, and also those who provided company or hospitality on recent trips to Continental Europe, particularly, in 2005, to Denmark, Estonia, Finland, twice to Italy, and four times to France. I am most grateful to Melissa Pine, Bill Purdue and John Young for their comments on part of an earlier draft, and to David Lidington and Warwick Lightfoot for discussing the subject with me. The book is dedicated to a fellow history student at university, who ably shared my interest in debating and has since had a distinguished public career.

CHAPTER 1

INTRODUCTION: TURNING POINTS AND CONTINGENCIES

The language of political debate is suffused with references to natural interest and inevitable destinies. That indeed is characteristic of much of the discussion favouring British engagement with the European Union. The standard theme is that Britain should fulfil its destiny to be at the heart of Europe, the latter a phrase that directly reflects the dominance of organic theories of community and statehood. For example, in 2002, Tony Blair told the Labour Party conference, 'The Euro is not just about our economy, but our destiny. We should only join the Euro if the economic tests are met. That is clear. But if the tests are passed we go for it', an approach that left little scope for equivocation or negotiation over terms. Furthermore, the language and the response of the faithful (not, by any means, all of the Labour Party) very much conformed to the leader principle that Blair utilized. Able to discern the truth of circumstances and the path to the future, he passed on his wisdom to mankind in a distinctly visionary fashion.

The obvious correlate of such language, particularly the heady reference to destiny, not exactly a divisible commodity, or one used with the suggestion of debate, is the argument that those who are foolish enough to disagree have a view that is made instantly redundant by their failure to understand interests and appreciate destinies. In short, their lack of an awareness of the deep rhythms of history is apparent, whereas that awareness, however, is vouchsafed to those who are correct. Revelation thus serves as a substitute for analysis.

This is an approach that is both insistent and insinuating. It is typical of Blair, but is also characteristic of much modern discussion, with its repeated preference for emotion over reason, for commitment over consideration, for discourse over analysis. This is also an approach that is wrong, as an assessment of the European question, of British interests, and as an understanding of historical processes. Far from there being any long-term inevitability in politics or political structures, or indeed, a totally clear-cut character to national identity and interests, such determinism dramatically fails to understand both the role of contingencies, and the place of particular conjunctures, in accounting for developments. This can be highlighted with reference to the past, present and future nature of Anglo-European relations, and this provides a necessary context for any discussion of the situation facing Britain and Europe today.

In practice, the interdependability that is frequently asserted did not, and does not, dictate the contours and consequences of the relationship, neither in general, nor with specific reference to Anglo-European relations. Choices on the content and implementation of policy existed, and exist, and indeed will continue to exist. This, however, has long been denied by politicians and polemicists keen to advocate a particular point of view, and to claim destiny or inevitability for it. These claims reflect not only the rhetoric of politics, but also historical and political imaginations that are inherently deterministic and/or authoritarian. In part, this argument is a product of teleological arguments that claim to detect a pattern in history, and a consequence of the dominance, since the nineteenth century, of organic theories of the community and their extrapolation onto Europe. As such, the European project is fundamentally ahistorical, for its assertions clash with the human scepticism that is integral to scholarly research, analysis and discussion.

The inherent authoritarianism of these organic theories and of the European cause, with its belief in a self-evident and objective political meaning or 'project', leaves no real space for individual free will, and scant room for those who do not concur. Indeed, the latter are essentially pathogens in such an approach, their views negative or subversive, and therefore dangerous and unhealthy. In short, these teleological concepts are essentially anti-democratic notions, whether Europe is understood as state, community, people or peoples.[1] This is precisely because a clear 'project' for continuing integration is conceived of as necessary and inevitable, and opposition, indeed criticism, stigmatized as anti-European.

These anti-democratic notions flow from a conviction that European union is necessary and desirable, and that it represents the way to ensure peace and prosperity, and to confirm survival, in a competitive international, and troubling domestic environment. As a consequence of this belief, Euro-enthusiasts discern a clear difference in the moral quality of the two sides in any debate over union, and this is linked to the idea that opponents are sufferers from false consciousness. Democracy, in this approach, intrudes not as a way to debate options, but rather to validate the correct choice, in what is very much a descending theory of government. Indeed, as the history of the European 'project' repeatedly demonstrates, if the correct choice is not made, this is a product of the failure of the voters and the electoral system, and a demonstration of both. Failure, therefore, is unacceptable, as the nature of progress is clear-cut.

The refusal of governments, such as those of Austria, Finland and Greece, to hold referenda on the European constitution, which they supported, before the plan was in fact interrupted by the negative views of the French and Dutch electorates is indicative, both of the situation in the early 2000s and, more generally, of the European 'project'. The constitution indeed was ratified by parliamentary means, rather than referenda, in Austria, Belgium, Cyprus, Germany, Greece, Hungary, Italy, Latvia, Lithuania, Malta, Slovakia and Slovenia. Under the federal constitution, a referendum in Germany is not permitted, a response to Hitler's use of populism; and the government refused to amend the federal constitution to enable the people to express their view. The fundamental nature of the change entailed by the constitution could not be trusted to popular debate and the direct consent of a referendum. Also indicative is the literature produced by the European Parliament on the issue. Instead of providing a basis for public debate about the value of the constitution, it explicitly argues the case for it, assuming that the benefits are obvious.

The processes by which senior European politicians gain power also frequently involve patronage or horse-trading, rather than direct election, as was shown when Dominique de Villepin, who had never run for elected office, but was a trusted protégé of Jacques Chirac, the French President, was appointed French Prime Minister by Chirac in May 2005. It is scarcely surprising that such ministers show little interest in defending public accountability when they attend European summits or the Council of Ministers. The democratic deficit is institutionally convenient, politically necessary, and personally appropriate for such individuals.

This approach can become more pointed if national electorates or governments dissent from the views of the non-integrationists. This was demonstrated, respectively, before the constitution debate, when the EU responded to the advance of the far-right as a result of success in Austrian elections (a position not taken towards its advance in other, more powerful European countries), and also in Chirac's hostile response to 'New Europe's' willingness to offer public support for the USA over the Middle East in 2003. Alongside the problem of senior national politicians playing such a role, comes that of failed, or disgraced, politicians sent to pastures new in Brussels. British commissioners have included those rejected by the electorate – Neil Kinnock and Chris Patten; as well as those whose political and governmental behaviour in Britain has been judged inappropriate – Leon Brittan and Peter Mandelson. Jacques Barrot, the French Transport Commissioner appointed in 2005, had a suspended prison sentence for embezzlement quashed by amnesty, the result all too typical of French politics.

The notion of criticism of the EU as stemming from false consciousness may seem as ridiculous as the dodgy history that supporters of the European 'project' often resort to, but words count. Furthermore, teleological assumptions have an impact, not only in the interpretative drive of spreading EU competence, but also in the repressive response to critics that is a necessary adjunct to securing acquiescence. For example, the European Arrest Warrant, which came into force on 1 January 2004, greatly eases extradition proceedings, not least because, while it remains the case that someone cannot be extradited if their alleged offence is not a crime in Britain, this is waived for offences including xenophobia and racism. While presented as a crucial aid against terrorism, an aid in bilateral relations that should not be dependent on the EU, the opportunity this presents for thought-policing, indeed, possibly in the future, the muzzling of debate on European matters, is immense.

Of course, as with laws against gun-ownership, such provisions largely deter the moderate and law-abiding, while offering only limited discouragement to the extremists and the violent. The pattern of politics across much of the EU is becoming one of EU government as a whole: a centre of a certain type seeks all power and makes it difficult for moderate opposition to stand any chance; and this, unfortunately, leads to a rise in extremism that is taken to validate the authoritarianism of this centre. The rise of fascist or fascistic political groupings in the EU, not least in such key integrationist EU states as Belgium, France, Germany and Italy, is not some unexpected by-product of its dominant political practice, but rather a consequence of how it operates. In some cases there are suggestions that this is deliberate. François Mitterrand, the French President from 1981 to 1994, appears to have fostered the rise of the National Front in France in order to weaken the Gaullists, and thus strengthen his hold on power, while his successor, Jacques Chirac, found the choice between Le Pen and himself in the second round of the French presidential election in 2002 very useful. The nearest corollary in Britain so far is Blair's frequent attempt to de-legitimize the Conservatives by presenting them as extreme. Similarly, a report commissioned by the BBC's Board of Governors that appeared in January 2005 noted that it was not impartial on EU news.

Thus, to Euro-enthusiasts, the opposition is both anachronistic and extreme, each aspects of the other condition. Derek

Scott, economic adviser to Blair from 1997 to 2003, pointed out the dubious nature of Blair's method of argument:

'There was no attempt to argue why membership of the single currency was necessary in political terms let alone economic ones, just a series of assertions and red herrings... It is all too easy to be taken along by him in a series of superficially logical steps... Those opposed... are portrayed as being out of date, stupid or both, denying the "European dimension" to British history, buttressed by a variety of straw men...his lack of historical perspective was reinforced by New Labour's political strategy, including naïve attempts to emancipate itself from the past... But there are many problems that can't be understood or addressed without a grasp of their historical roots.'[2]

Instead of reason, Blair relied on assertion in argument and on a 'trust me' faith that focused on the charismatic character of his attempted presidency.

On the left, the attempt to discredit criticism is given another ratchet with the denial that Social Democrats can be Euro-sceptic. This is intended to discredit such opponents as redundant, indeed 'Old Labour' in British vocabulary, and indeed Michael Foot, Tony Benn and Barbara Castle were each prominent Euro-sceptics. Such a view fails to note the range and complexity of left-wing views, which include strong Social Democratic movements in Sweden and Denmark, as well as the divisions among French Socialists. Furthermore, a strong left-wing case can be made for the populist rejection of integrationism and centralization, also seen on the right, one that is in line with traditional left-wing views.[3] This case would argue that when power is close to the people, not only do they have a sense of identification, but also one of social solidarity that strengthens the quest for social justice. This nation-state, or localist, dimension could be further enhanced by reference to environmental awareness and sustainability, in order to bring in the Greens.

These arguments have not been satisfactorily addressed by

those who press for European-level solutions, a notion that asserts a false community, namely Europe, and then seeks to deny roles for ones that actually exist: co-operation between such communities is not the EU option; instead, direction is the solution. The left-wing Euro-sceptic case, one neglected by the bulk of the Labour Party, is of value to Conservatives, as it serves as a reminder of the breadth of British opposition to integration and thus the value of rejecting the typecasting of this opposition. The latter is necessary because, as with most political movements, there are sectarian Euro-sceptics and it is necessary in a democratic society to try to recruit support as widely as possible. For example, alongside nationalist and historical appeals against integration, it is also valuable to deploy universalist arguments focused on global identities and views of the future. These are not limited to left or right.

As an example of the rhetorical approach of Euro-enthusiasts, the Social Affairs Unit website carried on 7 June 2005 a piece by the talented Cambridge historian, Brendan Simms, in which he pressed the case for what he termed 'a European superpower under British leadership', whatever the latter means. In his argument, there was the customary clarity of those who back the European 'project' and a lack of any willingness to consider alternatives, as well as a marked assertiveness: 'The vision that Mr. Blair must articulate… Britain must become the Prussia of European unification… The way forward must be…'. Such language betokens an unwillingness to engage with complexities that is at once naïve and arrogant. It is unclear, for example, that other powers will accept a British-provided European general staff or, more generally, that a European superpower would serve British interests, or indeed any conception of the latter not framed in terms of European activism. Simms wishes that such a power should intervene in Belarus or the Middle East, and appears unconcerned about the issue of democratic consent to such a process. He suggests that 'when a European 9/11 or its equivalent takes place, Britain will be ready and the resulting momentum will generate the emotional, political and the military fusion which the process of European integration has lacked hitherto'. This, unfortunately, is an echo of authoritarians advocating totalitarianism as the response to crisis; shades indeed of the Reichstag fire, not that Simms shares those values.

Fortunately, the nearest we have come to a European 9/11 is the Madrid bombings, which were more deadly than those in London, and these scarcely support Simms' analysis. Indeed, the withdrawal of Spain from the 'coalition of the willing', as a result of the change of government following the election held soon after the bombings, underlines the extent to which the idea of a European superpower is only possible if national democratic consent and sovereign power are lost. The London bombings of 2005 were presented by the government as proof of the value of European co-operation, but they also demonstrated the consequences of how a British governmental system within the EU had found it difficult to defend national interests, not least as authority over issues such as border control and repatriation of illegal immigrants was attenuated. The Anti-Terrorism, Crime and Security Act, passed in December 2001, in the aftermath of the September 11 attacks in the USA, gave the government power to have those suspected of terrorism locked up without trial if they were not British. This was a breach in the principle that everyone should be treated equally under the law, and one that was criticized in the EU's annual report on human rights issued in January 2003. That report, however, failed to address adequately the challenge posed by terrorism. The crisis led the government to take a more critical line towards the European Convention on Human Rights. In January 2003, Blair, characteristically mentioning a policy prospect first on the television, in this case *Breakfast with Frost*, suggested that, in his quest to restrict the number of asylum seekers, it might be necessary to look at British obligations under the Convention. Typically, the challenge was not faced.

It was left to the Conservatives to raise it in 2005, when Michael Howard proposed stricter control over immigration and asylum as a major policy commitment for the 2005 election. In response to these proposals from a major political party, Friso Rosco Abbing, the chief spokesman for the EU

Justice Commissioner, declared that they contravened Union laws to which Britain, he claimed, was bound. As a result, in effect, political proposals were to be constrained within the parameters established by the EU. They were not, indeed, in Abbing's view to be offered to the electorate.

One of the themes of this book is that Blair's naïvety about Europe in part rests on a consistent lack of understanding of national history, not only that of Britain but also those of other European states. This is also seen with Simms' piece which takes 1707 and 1866 as models for European integration. This rests, however, on a selective reading of both episodes. The Union of 1707 between England/Wales and Scotland in part rested on a determination not to be shut out from the English and colonial market: the Scottish economy was in a poor state, and this had been emphasized by the crushing failure of the Darien Scheme to establish a Scottish commercial entrepôt near Panama, while, conversely, the strengthening pull of the London market had a growing effect on the Scottish economy. Yet, there were other reasons as well, which Simms fails to discuss. Political problems and personal opportunism were the most important. The civil war of 1689-91 had underlined the divisions in Scottish society, and made rule from London seem more attractive than government by Scottish opponents. In practice, the powerful leadership of the Presbyterian Church, fearful of exiled Stuarts and Scottish Episcopalians, accepted the Union as a political necessity. The passage of Union through the Scottish Parliament ultimately depended on successful political management, corruption and self-interest. Simms sees this as a model, but it was an incorporating, not a confederal, union. In 1708, the Scottish Privy Council, the executive agency for Scotland, was abolished without consultation. The governmental implications for England were far less important, because it was the more populous and wealthier of the two states that dominated the new British political system. The political consequences, however, were distinctly unhappy: a large number of Scottish Protestants rejected the new order to the extent that they were willing to rebel in 1715, albeit without success.

The role of force in the Anglo-Scottish Union was replicated in Germany. Simms appears to wish to ignore the extent to which this rested on war between the German states. Bavarians, Hanoverians and others proved willing to fight against Prussian invasion in 1866. It was Prussian military success that explained unification, not a wellspring of popular support, a point that German nationalists were keen to ignore. Simms appears to assume that German Unification was a clear bonus for the Germans, without at least considering the argument that it helped to propel them into two disastrous wars which led in 1945 to the occupation of the entire country. In this context, 'the determination of the smaller German states not to surrender their hard-won sovereignty' was prescient, and a more useful analogy for modern Europe than the lesson in favour of unification that Simms draws.

Aside from offering a dodgy history that neglects different strands of British national development, advocates for a European identity for Britain also suffer from a conceptual failure to understand the possible relationship between similarity, the apparent goal of Euro-convergence, and continued rivalry. Comparisons may be used to detect similarities, but affinity between Britain (and other countries) and their neighbours is not the only reason for closeness, co-operation or union. Complementarity is also at issue. It, indeed, was the basis of the economic relationships of the British Empire, which relied on mutually-profitable differences in production. This situation helped to make British adjustment to the European Economic Community (EEC) difficult, because in place of the Empire, with its controlled exchange economy designed for mutual benefit, Britain was offered, thanks to similarities with her neighbours, a union of competitors rather than of partners. Britain competed as an industrial exporter and agricultural producer, particularly with France, Germany and Italy, and this competition hit important sections of the British economy. Thus, similarity and convergence are not necessarily the best conditions for unity.

In place of a deterministic, or over-determined, account about Europe's development, should come an awareness of indeterminacy and a lack of inevitability. This stems from a number of sources and can be seen at play on a variety of scales, most particularly Britain, Continental Europe, Anglo-European relations, and the wider international sphere. Indeterminacy also arises from contested identities, for example the longstanding tension in Germany between a confidence in the West, that entails looking to Britain and the USA, and, instead, an emphasis on a supposedly European or Christian identity or set of values. The latter approach is more sympathetic to closer relations with France and integration within the EU.

The sources of indeterminacy are also varied, necessarily so, as factors that pertain in wartime are different to peacetime counterparts. For example, much of the history of Europe over the last six decades, including the formation of what became the European Union, stems from World War Two. That conflict underlined an important degree of British exceptionalism, with Britain being the sole European opponent of Germany throughout the war. Britain was also the only country that did not suffer occupation: the Soviet Union, which anyway was allied to Germany in 1939-41, was also undefeated, but much of it was occupied, while, for Britain, only the Channel Isles suffered a similar fate. Yet any reading of the crisis accompanying and following the defeat makes it clear that other scenarios were possible, not least a negotiated settlement in 1940 that left Britain a complicit ally, like Vichy France, or, less plausibly but still possibly, a successful German invasion of Britain that year.

In peacetime, indeterminacy is a natural and necessary product of democratic politics, as elections provide opportunities for the electorate to choose between distinct parties and their policies. A reminder of this unpredictability was brought to the fore in 2002 when Gerhard Schröder, the unpopular Chancellor, unexpectedly won re-election by only 10,000 votes. In large part, this was due to two unexpected events. First, Schröder's opposition to Anglo-American policy over Iraq won him support, particularly in formerly Communist East Germany. Secondly, serious floods in East Germany won more support as he responded promptly with substantial financial assistance. In 2005, Angela Merkel's weakness as the CDU candidate against Schröder added a new source of uncertainty.

Indeterminacy can also be seen in Britain, and many of the contingencies in play can be related to European consequences, or even causes. The elections in 1964 and February 1974 were both particularly close, while the results in 1970 and 1992 were unexpected by many commentators. Given Labour's divisions on the EEC, it is likely that although a victory for Wilson in 1970 would have still led to a resumption of negotiations for entry, there might well have been more of a reluctance to surrender national interests than was to be seen under Heath. Had the latter still been Prime Minister in 1975 there would have been no referendum on continued membership, as he epitomized the democratic deficit. Labour victory in 1992 would have left Labour to bear the burden of the 1990s recession and the Maastricht debate. This would have helped the Conservatives to return to power in 1997, if not earlier, and the context would have permitted them to adopt a more robustly national line than was to be taken by Major in office. Defeat in 1992 would probably have led to the fall of the latter.

The electoral system could also have changed, as the parties of the centre-Liberals, Social Democrats and, later, Liberal Democrats demanded, producing the 'realignment' of British politics pressed for in the SDP's founding Limehouse Declaration in 1981. Labour's failure in the Euro-elections in 1999, the first national election in Britain under a system of proportional representation (and a demonstration of the pressure for change that stemmed from the EU), led Blair to abandon his commitment to holding a referendum on proportional representation before the next general election. Had such a system been introduced then, or earlier, it is likely that all governments would have been coalitions, and probable therefore, that centrist tendencies would have been dominant. This might well have had consequences in terms of European policy.

When, in defiance of this role of contingency, commentators refer to deterministic outcomes, they are often indulging in polemic designed to influence the political debate; but all too frequently they also betray an unhappiness with the reality of democratic mandates and contempt for the concept and contents of popular and, even more, populist politics. This indeed represents a fundamental divide between Continental European states and Britain. In the Continental states, there is the concept and reality of what Helmut Schmidt, Chancellor of Germany from 1974 to 1982, termed the 'political class', a notion integral to the theory and practice of government in the EEC, and now the EU. It can also be seen in France where a small elite of graduates of the *grandes écoles*, particularly the Ecole Polytechnique and the Ecole Nationale d'Administration, established in 1945, dominated government, politics and business through a system of *pantouflage*. Chirac is an ENA graduate, as is Giscard d'Estaing and prime ministers such as Fabius from the left and Juppé from the right. A disinclination to accept public scrutiny and, therefore, accountability was seen in many EU institutions. Thus, the European Central Bank, which was established in 1998, refused to publish the minutes of the meetings of its Governing Council or to record any votes taken at these meetings.

This approach contrasts with the theory of British politics, with its emphasis on a more democratized practice of politics. The latter has more in common with the politics of the USA, than those of many Continental states. However, the combination of government authoritarianism, legal pretension, and the effects of minority governments elected under the first-past-the-post system, in the context of three major parties and declining electoral participation, with a smaller percentage of the vote and of the electorate, is lessening the democratic character of political practice in Britain.

The nature of government in the EU is a process of spin. Again Britain, under the Blair governments from 1997, has considerably relied on spin, but, within the EU, this spin has been greatly institutionalized. In 2005, the European Communications Commissioner, Margot Wallstrom, advanced what she termed 'ten concrete actions' designed to ensure that the EU constitution was ratified throughout the EU. These included massive expenditure on propaganda, and its institutionalization in a manner that would facilitate such future campaigns. 'Public information' for the campaign included Europe direct call centres whose arguments were scarcely to be unbiased: to 'explain to the public how the constitution will benefit them in their everyday lives'. The constitution proposed to take this further by giving the right to stop funding political parties, and this is linked to the obligation on the latter to further 'European awareness'. The notion that the parties might represent people and, on that basis, however unwelcome, should be encouraged to take part in debate, was understandably not attractive because of the belief that the political class takes precedence in the EU vision. Thus, in order to try to meet the Maastricht Treaty criteria, the Juppé government in France (Juppé was Prime Minister under Chirac in 1995-7) introduced the measures intended to cut government spending by decree, and not via parliament.

In the EU, it is indeed 'us' and 'them' politics, except that the nature of the governmental structure created by the EU is inherently anti-political, in so far as politics is to be understood not only as a popular process but also one in which different views may be legitimately accepted. As such, the EU, while speaking of progress, and having a parliament to monitor the Commission and the Council of Ministers, is inherently controlling, potentially coercive, and fundamentally illiberal and reactionary. For these reasons, the notion of a renegotiation of the terms of Britain's relations with the EU is flawed, as it is unclear that there is any willingness on the part of the EU Commission or Britain's fellow-members to accept the practice of such renegotiation.

Differences between Britain and the Continent will emerge in this work, but before turning to them, it is necessary to emphasize that once inevitability is discarded, as both means and content, and as both analysis of the past and prospectus for the future, then it becomes possible to discuss matters without foreclosing the options. That is the democratic method, one that all too many commentators prove unwilling to accept.

1 See also L. Siedentop, *Democracy in Europe* (London, 2001).
2 D. Scott, *Off Whitehall. A View from Downing Street by Tony Blair's Adviser* (London, 2004).
3 A. Forster, *Euroscepticism in Contemporary British Politics: Opposition to Europe in the British Conservative and Labour Parties since 1945* (London, 2002).

CHAPTER 2

DEEP HISTORY: BRITAIN AND EUROPE, THE HISTORICAL BACKGROUND

To understand the European question, it is necessary to look at the past, a past unwisely neglected by those with a fixation on their concept of the future. This chapter looks at the long-term nature of the relationship between Britain and Continental Europe prior to the foundation of the European Economic Community under the Treaty of Rome signed on 25 March 1957. Taking effect from 1 January 1959, this treaty was the background to the current European Union. The chapter will provide a brief survey of developments, and use them to indicate the complexities of European history, not least the degree to which common elements, such as the Classical and Christian inheritances, led within Europe to very different political and social arrangements and attitudes. The causes and nature of British exceptionalism, the extent to which the country was different to Europe, and that this interacted with unique political characteristics, have to be examined with care. Particular emphasis needs to be placed on Britain's global position, and on the degree to which this led not only to a profound 'functional difference' between Britain and Continental Europe, in terms, for example, of the importance of trans-oceanic trade and empire to Britain, but also to a more lasting cultural and ideological inheritance of difference. The democratic character of British political culture also requires consideration.

Much of the debate on Britain's role in Europe is ahistorical, in that it takes particular episodes, using them to support or criticize a notion of inherent engagement, and fails either to engage with the methodological perspective noted in the last chapter, or with the need to locate particular examples in their multiple contexts. Conceptually, there is also the problem that Europe is taken to be an entity within which or with which Britain can be readily compared or contrasted. There is a lack of understanding, instead, of the extent to which Europe has always been diverse in circumstances and culture, with, furthermore, particular issues of definition in border zones. For example, to see allegiance to the Catholic Church as the definition of medieval Europe makes little sense from the perspective of Byzantine (Greek Orthodox) Europe, which included much of Eastern Europe, nor from that of pagan Lithuania. The trajectory of regional, national and European development also looks very different, both in the past and today, from across Europe. This is the case whether the vista is from Malmo, Madrid, Munich or Milan, and, from that perspective, Manchester or Middlesbrough simply adds another exceptionalism, rather than proving unusual in their uniqueness. This is a point possibly better understood in Montrose or Merioneth due to the emphasis of Scottish and Welsh nationalists on a 'Europe of the regions'.

During its history, Britain, or large parts of it, has been a central part of a trans-Channel polity. This was the case, to a varying extent, from the Norman Conquest in 1066 until the loss of Calais in 1558. England and Wales were more tangential parts of the Roman Empire. Most recently, such a link existed with the Electorate of Hanover, under the rulers of the House of Hanover, in 1714-1837. Furthermore, close and important relations with Continental Europe have been a major theme of English, Scottish, Welsh, Irish and British history. Yet, that implies neither uniformity nor even, necessarily, a strong degree of European identity.

In addition, the theses of British exceptionalism, and of Britain's close contacts with the Continent over the centuries, are not incompatible, for identity is neither exclusive nor a constant. Instead, with the political community the product of more than one imagination, a sense of collective self-awareness can include a number of levels or aspects of identification. Moreover, these often develop, or are expressed most clearly, in hostility or opposition to other groups, and their real or imagined aims and attributes, and these groups are frequently ones with which relations are close, particularly physically so. Indeed, this closeness is almost necessarily the case. As a result, the reality of overlapping senses of collective self-awareness can be very difficult, as also can be the processes of often continued adaptation in these senses. Thus, senses of identity are more amorphous, changeable and, at the same time, atavistic and negative than the secular positivism implied by any stress on constitution-making, such as the discussion on the future of the EU. To move from the abstract, English and, later, British self-identity owed much to hostility to, or at least competition with, important parts of Continental Europe.

The European myth that the EU represents and propagates entails anachronism, teleology and reification. In short, it is an echo of the national myths that have played such a major role in the creation of nation-states. These myths, however, were grounded in the experience of particular political communities or nations; they have, over much of Europe, particularly in Britain and, even more, England, had centuries to work; they can look back on a history of military and political challenges that have been confronted and often surmounted; and they are lent force by the institutions of states that reach into every community and life, for example through education. In many states, language also provides a powerful unifier. In contrast, none of these circumstances is true of the European myth.

For most of the post-Roman period until the French Revolution, the nearest equivalent term to Europe was Christendom. However much the present myth of Europe requires such an anachronism, Christendom should not be seen as a proto-Europe. For Christendom, belief, not place, counted as a basis for loyalty and identity, and this is abundantly clear in the modern world, with Christendom extending far beyond Europe. The role of faith ensured that Christendom had a shared ideology that was more potent than anything modern Europe possesses. Furthermore, although the rift between Roman and Greek Christianity was a serious division within each zone, episcopal and parochial structures gave Christendom an organization lacking in modern Europe.

Other institutions, such as preaching orders, supplemented this strength.

Alongside the wide-ranging and unifying strand offered by Christendom, the kingdoms created by the 'Barbarian' invaders of the Roman Empire provided the basis for subsequent senses of identity within Western Europe, in a way that the governmental logic provided by the provinces of the Roman Empire had been unable to do. The subsequent cohesion of the English state was readily apparent, after the abrupt discontinuity created by the Norman Conquest in 1066, in large part because the Normans and their Angevin successors built on the Anglo-Saxon inheritance. As a result, there was a marked contrast with the stronger aspect of feudalism in France.

At the same time, there were also important developments over the centuries that followed the Norman Conquest, and these helped provide a further distinctive character to English society and politics. These included the role of the Common Law, the growing use of the vernacular (the English language), the development of Parliament, and the increased flexibility of English society. The Common Law was an important aspect of English distinctiveness, and, from the twelfth century, this was true of both the content of the law and the way in which it was administered; and that at a time when Roman law was coming back into fashion on the Continent. English Common Law was particularly suited to the protection of rights and liberties, and it encouraged a respect for the autonomy of individual thought and action. In combination with the early emergence of an institutional monarchy, this was particularly responsible for the character and continuity of English political society. There was more public law than in areas on the Continent where feudalism had made more of an impact, and more of a sense of equality under the law.

The development of the vernacular also had a political aspect. At the start of the Hundred Years' War in the 1330s, the aristocracy of England was international in outlook and French was the language at the royal court and of anyone with upwardly mobile aspirations. However, as politics drove the two realms into a long war, it became awkward that high society in England aped French style, manners and customs. The government also manipulated patriotic characteristics and deliberately harnessed linguistic awareness. In 1344, it was claimed before the House of Commons, an important and indicative choice of location, that Philip VI of France was 'fully resolved...to destroy the English language, and to occupy the land of England'. As the lower classes spoke English anyway, it was only a shift by the upper classes that was at issue.

The common strand of Christendom itself was fragmented and greatly altered during the so-called early-modern period of the sixteenth and seventeenth centuries, thanks to the Reformation, the development of state mechanisms and ideologies, the further rise of vernacular languages, and the creation of trans-oceanic empires. These changes did not contribute to a concept of Europe that meant much as far as its peoples and governments were concerned; indeed they greatly lessened it in practice and theory. Instead, in England the national consciousness, nationalism and unitary state that can already be seen in the fifteenth century as a result of medieval developments became stronger in the sixteenth. Furthermore, a self-conscious cultural nationalism became far more apparent, despite an emphasis on a common Protestantism. Similar processes occurred elsewhere.

The French Revolutionary and Napoleonic period (1789-1815), on the other hand, witnessed not only a political struggle that absorbed the whole of the Continent, but also the formulation of universalist revolutionary and counter-revolutionary ideologies. The language of politics changed radically, and the basic configuration of internal political struggles for the nineteenth century was therefore established. The universalist, and somewhat utopian, language of the French Revolutionary period offered an alternative ideology to the nation-state, but, in practice, it was suffused with social division, political violence and French self-interest.

Instead of dwelling on the French Revolution, the EU, in creating an apparently exemplary history to anchor its teleological mission, has preferred to look back to the eighteenth-century European Enlightenment, presenting it as a worthy precursor of its goals, and, indeed, a movement with progressive and tolerant values. The Enlightenment, however, also offers troubling parallels with the modern stage of European history, as well as an instructive contrast with the situation in eighteenth-century Britain. Whereas the cultural and intellectual life of the latter was broad-based, and rested on considerable, and legally-grounded, political and religious freedom, the situation was different across most of Europe, with the exception of the United Provinces (modern Netherlands) and Hamburg. In contrast to the situation in Britain, most of the Continental Enlightenment was top-down and only shallowly rooted in public support. This helped account for important facets of its character (although, lacking an organizational structure, the Enlightenment was particularly diverse) as self-righteous and socially condescending. The populace were generally presented by Enlightenment ministers and commentators as ignorant, and their beliefs treated as the very antithesis of those of the Enlightened. The peasantry (the bulk of the population) were to be improved, in spite of themselves, and the language used to describe them was that used to discuss children, the mentally weak, or animals. Prefiguring much of modern European political culture, the intellectuals, who sought to influence Enlightenment governments, dismissed what they disliked as superstitious, exaggerated the possibilities of change through education, and neglected the difficulties of turning aspirations into policies, as well as the problems of government, the vitality of popular religiosity, and the disinclination of people to subordinate self-interest, and their own notions of a just society, to the views and self-righteousness of others.

This popular neglect of the path to a just society helped, however, to produce frustration and confusion among some 'progressive' thinkers during the early years of the French Revolution. This frustration, indeed, engendered an attitude in which the creation and defence of a just society through terror seemed necessary, again a marked contrast with contemporary

British society. In short, just as Romanticism ultimately led to Hitler – not that his policies accorded with the assumptions of Romantic thinkers – so the Enlightenment led to the French Revolutionary Terror of 1793-4, with those who lacked the necessary virtue treated as public enemies as the guillotine went about its abrupt labours.

France also overran and dominated much of Europe between 1792 and 1813, prefiguring the experience with Germany in the twentieth century, and this helped ensure in Britain a marked degree of exceptionalism and a self-conscious note of difference from the Continent. The French Revolutionaries created sister republics of the well-intentioned, for example the Batavian Republic out of the United Provinces. In practice, however, these states were based both on a narrow fragment of local support – only the virtuous were allowed power – and also had to serve the military and international goals of the Revolution. Indeed, the compulsory virtue of the entire project is uncomfortably reminiscent of European integrationist attitudes today, not least with its teleological confidence in the project, and the sense that the ends justified the means.

As with earlier opposition to Louis XIV of France (r. 1643-1715), Britain played its major role in resisting the challenges posed by French expansionism, alongside other powers, but only Russia shared Britain's ability to avoid defeat and occupation, and, for Russia, this ability was scarcely evident on the battlefield of Austerlitz in 1805, or as Moscow fell to Napoleon in 1812. Both powers were, in a way, outside Europe: able, to a considerable extent, to protect their home base or centres of power from other European states, yet also able to play a major part in European power politics. In almost every respect, however, whether social, economic, religious or political, the differences between Britain and Russia were vast, and their earlier and later histories were very different. Thus, their geopolitical similarity at this juncture, in marked contrast to the rest of Europe, is a caution against assuming that, in all criteria, Britain was closest to nearby parts of Europe, and also against putting too great a stress on apparently consistent parallel developments, as opposed to more short-term convergences and divergences, or, indeed, alliances of expediency, such as that between Britain and the Soviet Union in 1941-5.

Britain played a major role in organizing and financing Continental opposition to France from 1793 to 1815. However, despite the aspirations of counter-revolutionaries such as, most vocally, Edmund Burke in the early 1790s, this was not really a matter of France against Europe with Britain playing a key role in the latter. Instead, prefiguring the situation in Europe between 1939 and 1944, what was striking was how much the Continental powers were prepared to co-operate with the French, including accepting the consequences of defeat and even fighting Britain. This was true, for example, of Spain from 1796 to 1808, just as it was to be true of Germany and Vichy France in 1940-2. Indeed, Napoleon was able to bully much of Continental Europe into the Continental Blockade of Britain declared in 1806. This was a form of economic warfare very much based on the idea that Britain was separate from the rest of Europe. In some respects, this was a wartime anticipation of the peacetime bloc that the EEC represented prior to British entry.

The Napoleonic period also saw Britain greatly extend her power outside Europe, at the expense both of other European powers – France, Spain and the Dutch – and of non-European states. At the same time, another type of distinctiveness stemmed from Britain's swelling economy and, even more, from the economic transformation of the country which made Britain the power-house and financial centre of the world. Comparisons then were scarcely pertinent with much of Europe. The French Revolution and Napoleonic Wars anticipated World War Two in underlining and accentuating British distinctiveness as far as the rest of Europe was concerned, but were very different in one particular respect: World War Two, like World War One, gravely weakened Britain, while the USA emerged as the dominant power; whereas the wars of 1792-1815 had seen Britain become even more dominant as the world's leading naval and commercial power. Indeed, for the

USA, these wars were principally of value in permitting a period of consolidation without serious interruption by the European powers.

When peace came for Britain in 1815, its commerce was in a uniquely powerful situation. By the 1820s, the British economy was growing at 2 per cent per year, a rate that might seem low now, but that contrasted with the stasis generally characteristic of agrarian societies. The harnessing of technological change contributed to an economic transformation of the country, as did the benefits of readily available capital, an increasingly productive agricultural sector, and the burgeoning markets of a growing home and colonial population. In 1820-4, the annual averages of coal and lignite production, a crucial ingredient of industrialization, in million metric tonnes, were eighteen for Britain and two for France, Germany, Belgium and Russia combined.

Yet, from the 1830s, imperial expansion and economic growth were to follow rapidly in other parts of Western Europe – France, indeed, capturing Algiers in 1830. This was sufficiently so to ensure that, by 1870, there was considerable similarity between Britain and much of Western Europe. A good index was provided by the key modernizing transport technology of the period – railways. In 1870, Britain had the densest rail network in Europe, a reflection of British innovation, expertise, capital and demand, but France, Germany, the Low Countries and northern Italy also had a fairly dense network by then. These networks contrasted with regions with fewer rail lines, particularly Iberia, southern Italy, and Eastern Europe, and also with those with no lines, most obviously the bulk of the Balkans. Thus, the coming of rail replicated, although not precisely, some earlier economic changes, in that North-West Europe, including Britain, displayed similar characteristics.

Yet, there were also major economic differences between Britain and Continental Europe that were more widely significant, prefiguring contrasts that have remained important in recent decades. Britain traded abroad far more than the Continental countries, and far more widely. Her major industrial sectors, textiles and metal products, were dependent on exports. Continental economies were more self-sufficient; what foreign trade they did was mainly with other European countries (including Britain). As a result, Britain was dependent on foreign trade, and on the wider world outside Europe, in a way that they were not. This dependency was related to other aspects of Britain's distinctiveness: her outward-lookingness and internationalism; her interest in peace, which was believed to create the best conditions for trade; and her opposition to a large and expensive army, and also to compulsory military service. Both were seen as products of authoritarianism and as likely to sustain a state power judged unacceptable to the political libertarianism of British society.

In the political sphere, there were also important parallels between Britain and the Continent. Democratization, urbanization and mass literacy combined to ensure a stronger political consciousness across Europe. Yet, nationalism, not internationalism, was the key political form of identity and commitment. Britain experienced social and cultural developments similar to those on the Continent, sharing, for example, in a general secularization and a measure of religious disestablishment, as well as in the co-existence of a hierarchical society with rapid social changes. Throughout Europe, including Britain, there were significant transformations, both cause and consequence of societies with increasing education and political rights, and widespread urbanization and industrialization. These changes brought social dislocation, instability and anxiety, which was expressed in part, in Britain, as on the Continent, by hostility to immigrants. More generally, on both sides of the Channel, and prefiguring changes since 1945, deference and traditional social patterns ebbed. Privilege co-existed with meritocratic notions, and greatly expanded institutions that, within limits, reflected the latter: the civil service, the professions, the public schools, the universities, and the armed forces all played a role in the creation of a new social and cultural establishment different from the traditional aristocracy. Similarly, working-class political consciousness and activism developed in both Britain and the Continent.

Whatever the similarities, however, British society, political culture and politics retained an important sense of distinction. The perfectibility, or perfection, of the British constitution was asserted and widely believed in, with reform legislation and spreading imperial power contributing to an optimistic conception of past, present and future, linked together in a utilitarian liberalism. Extensions of the franchise from 1832 were seen as arising naturally from the country's development and political culture. There were also significant differences between British and Continental political movements. British Liberalism was neither republican nor socialist, and its leadership came from within the governing elite. Furthermore, the British Labour/Socialist movement was very much on the periphery of the Second International: Marxism was decidedly weak in Britain compared with most Continental countries. By Continental standards, the Liberal Party was particularly popular, and its Conservative rival notably liberal.

Nevertheless, even if political, legal and institutional traditions separated Britain from Continental states, they had problems in common. Although similar social and economic trends impacted upon different cultures, there were common transformations in the fabric of life.

Yet, the largely peaceful situation in England, Scotland and Wales, but not Ireland, contrasted with the bitter divisions in nineteenth-century Belgian, French, German, Italian, Portuguese and Spanish society, and their recent histories of internal conflict and revolution, that made it far harder to imagine for these countries a convincing positive account of long-term and unitary national development. Instead, their modern foundation myths were accounts of authoritarian direction or popular activism overcoming sectional opposition. Victorian Britain indeed displayed a sense of national uniqueness, nationalistic self-confidence and xenophobic contempt for foreigners. This xenophobia, however, was not a matter of hostility to foreigners *per se*, but rather a reaction to what was seen as backward and illiberal. Backwardness and illiberality were defined in accordance with British criteria, but these criteria were also seen as of wider applicability.

Whatever their interest in Empire, and indeed, in part, in response to it, British governments took a close interest in developments on the Continent. The concepts of the 'Balance of Power' from the eighteenth century, and the 'Concert of Europe' in the nineteenth, indicate how central the Continent was in the conduct of British foreign policy. Furthermore, as also earlier, at Utrecht in 1713, and later in 1919 and 1945, British ministers had played a crucial role in the peace settlement of 1815 agreed at the Congress of Vienna, and they were concerned about the fate of the settlement, and about other international developments. In addition, imperial issues could have a European dimension, most obviously with 'the Eastern Question' created by Turkish weakness and Russian ambitions in the Balkans and the Near East. British opposition to Russian expansion led to war, in the shape of the Crimean War (1854-6), and later to threats of conflict in the 1870s and 1880s. One crisis over the Turkish Empire led to the terms Jingoes and Jingoism as a result of a music-hall song by 'The Great Macdermott', the chorus of which started, 'We don't want to fight, but by jingo if we do, we've got the ships, we've got the men, we've got the money too.' This, however, represented a strategic concern about Turkey that prefigured NATO commitments to Turkey designed against Soviet expansion, and not the current interest in Turkish membership in, and therefore political influence over, the EU.

Britain was no more insulated economically than politically. Economic growth in Britain did not mean that there were no fears of Continental economic competition. At the same time, again prefiguring present differences and tensions, there was a tension over economic interests. Free trade played a major role in British policy and popular ideology, but this economic liberalism, although influential, struggled against protectionism on the Continent. For example, the Prussian-led German *Zollverein* (customs union), founded in 1834, imposed tariffs on British manufactured goods that led to frequent protests from British manufacturers and merchants.

Culturally, at least at the elite level, Britain was far closer to the Continent than today because, as yet, there was no focus on the USA. Educated Victorians were acutely aware of what they shared with their European counterparts as a result of a common culture based upon Christianity and the legacy of ancient Greece and Rome. Those who could afford to do so, performed and listened to German music, read French novels, and visited the art galleries of Italy. Travel to the Continent was regarded as a crucial aspect of a civilized upbringing. At the same time, as so often, an 'engagement' with the Continent meant, in practice, a construction of it in British terms, and a response by the British accordingly. This can be seen with music. British audiences heard much Continental music, but, before this is uncritically regarded as a sign of cosmopolitanism, it is necessary to note that the British celebrated their own nationality in this praise of foreign music. Composers who were willing to pander to British taste, such as Mendelssohn with his oratorios, were hits, while Verdi was popular in large part because he was seen as a liberal nationalist defying autocracy and the Papacy.

Economic success was important to national confidence. It was most developed in the 1850s and 1860s, which were abnormally prosperous decades, but even then it was not unqualified. Anticipating subsequent situations, moreover, there was also considerable anxiety, and these became more marked in the late-nineteenth century, not least with a rise in competition, particularly from Germany and the USA, and also in response to anxiety about the growing importance of organized labour. This led to a search for solutions that focused not on co-operation within Europe, but rather on national and imperial regeneration. The former lay behind the social welfarism of the 1900s, and the latter behind the campaign, led by Joseph Chamberlain, for an imperial tariff union that played such a major role in the same period. From both perspectives, Continental Europe was not the solution and, indeed, in some respects, for example German industrial development and, until the mid-1900s, French and Russian imperial competition, it was the clear problem.

Nevertheless, whatever the worries, not least rising German international and naval assertiveness, the situation at the outset of the twentieth century was more confident than it was to be a century later. In *The Economic Consequences of the Peace* (1919), John Maynard Keynes reflected on the pre-war era:

> 'What an extraordinary episode in the economic progress of man that age was which came to an end in August, 1914...life offered, at a low cost and with the least trouble... conveniences, comforts, and amenities beyond the compass of the richest and most powerful monarchs of other ages. The inhabitant of London could order by telephone, sipping his morning tea in bed, the various products of the whole earth...he could at the same moment and by the same means adventure his wealth in the natural resources and new enterprises of any quarter of the world...
> But, most important of all, he regarded this state of affairs as normal, certain, and permanent, except in the direction of further improvement, and any deviation from it as aberrant, scandalous, and avoidable.'

Globalism then particularly suited Britain, but the very dynamic capitalist world in which it played a key role was to be hit hard by World War One (1914-18). Entered into in order to preserve the balance of power in the face of German aggression, this was not a conflict that led to widespread respect, affection or support for Continental models and methods. Further challenges to the global order came from the Russian Revolution of 1917, which created a sense of threat in Britain – the Bolshevik menace – and also from the Great Depression of the 1930s, which led to a major increase in international protectionism and, in the case of Britain, to a greater stress on imperial trade. None of this took Britain closer to Continental Europe. Indeed, it was seen as the source of political and economic problems, and not as the solution. Nevertheless, the failure to produce a lasting international political settlement at Versailles in 1919 ensured that British Foreign Secretaries in the 1920s and 1930s devoted more time to Continental affairs than had been the case when major changes had been taking place there in the 1860s and 1870s, although the latter had not been neglected.

Some groups were very engaged with issues on the Continent. Ideologically those on the left who went to fight against Fascism during the Spanish Civil War (1936-9) were far distant from Sir Oswald Mosley and his fascist Blackshirts, but they shared a world-view in which developments in Britain could be understood in terms of those on the Continent, and vice versa. As such, they were different from the bulk of the population who wished very much to see Britain in isolation or within the context of the Empire, an approach very much taken when, first, Edward VIII and then George VI came to the throne in 1936.

Hostility to the nature and content of contemporary politics, and a search for new solutions to serious economic and political problems, led critics in both Britain and the Continent to turn to radical alternatives, Communism and Fascism, that were associated with foreign states. For the bulk of the population, however, geopolitical concerns about Soviet (Russian) or German intentions did not equate with any ideological commitment or europhilia. Cultural links, and parallels with Continental developments, were matched by differences and a strong sense of cultural nationalism. Among the differences was a widespread hostility on the Continent to parliamentarianism. This was seen with the rise of authoritarianism in most of Europe, not least Eastern Europe, Germany and the Mediterranean. It was also an issue in France. This contributed to the differing response between Britain and France when both were defeated by Germany in 1940.

In World War Two (1939-45), Britain's European alliance system rapidly collapsed. Winston Churchill's idea in 1940, as France succumbed to German invasion, of a union between Britain and France, was the desperate product of failure, not a considered response enjoying widespread support. Britain, instead, was excluded by defeat from a Continent which, to the west of the Soviet Union, had been brought under the hegemony of a single power, Germany, which was allied to the Soviet Union. Such a process was contested: London was the collecting house for governments in exile, and resistance activities played a role, but Britain had to turn to the Empire and the USA for help against Hitler. Indeed, in so far as European unification seemed a prospect in the early 1940s, it was a matter, as under Napoleon, not of the communalism of exiles in London, but of co-operation with the conqueror. Although this strand was subsequently to be largely ignored, part of the genesis of the European Union can be traced to the ideas and practices that focused on Vichy's collaboration with Nazi Germany. Indeed this issue was to dog the reputation of François Mitterrand, France's President from 1981 to 1995.

A different form of co-operation had been outlined by Hitler's Foreign Minister, Ribbentrop, when he was envoy in London. He had initially argued that an Anglo-German league based on racial affinity and anti-Communism was possible, a typical instance of the uneasy combination of national and supra-national forces and interests that was so important in the development of notions of European alliances. Such ideas, however, were rejected in 1940. The prospect of a negotiated peace with Hitler, that several prominent politicians, such as Halifax, the Foreign Secretary, and Lloyd George, who had met Hitler and who saw himself as a Prime Minister in waiting, were willing to support, was cut short when Churchill out-manoeuvred his rivals in the government.

This, indeed, was a key moment in Britain avoiding convergence with the Continent and, instead, defining itself as both separate and outward-looking, a moment that understandably plays a major role in the collective memory, and is shadowed by pressure, from Europhiles and German commentators, not to talk about the war. Instead, Britain chose to rely on the support of the Empire, particularly in 1940-1, and on the entry into the war, first, of the Soviet Union and, subsequently, of the USA. The limited affection the British displayed towards the French was a product not only of Vichy's willingness to co-operate with the Germans, but also of the difficulties created by the Free French under Charles de Gaulle. At the same time, concern about the spread of Communism led to British interest in the security of Eastern Europe, even if, in 1944-5, as in 1939 for Poland, 1940 for Finland, and 1941 for Yugoslavia and Greece, it was unable to give effect to its aspirations.

British plans for post-war Europe included military speculation about the need to ally with a rearmed Germany against the Soviet Union. At the same time, there was an awareness that Britain's relations with Continental Europe had been changed by the impact of the war, an impact also seen in shifts within the Anglo-American alliance as British influence and power diminished. The European world, and Britain with it, seemed weaker and indeed it was. As Jawaharlal Nehru pointed out, 'Europe is no longer the center of world affairs.'[1]

1 For a recent account of the historical background, K. Robbins, *Britain and Europe 1789-2005* (London, 2005).

CHAPTER 3

'JOINING EUROPE': BRITAIN AND EUROPE, THE HISTORICAL BACKGROUND

This chapter brings into focus the topics covered in the previous one by concentrating on the more specific questions: firstly, why Britain did not become a founder member of the European Economic Community (EEC) in the 1950s; secondly why it was kept out in the 1960s; thirdly, why it joined in 1973.

A consideration of Anglo-European relations today leads to a particular perspective on the past, not least the question of why Britain did not join the EEC as seeming the big issue when considering the late 1940s and 1950s. In large part, however, this is a poorly-posed question, because most commentators in the late 1940s did not foresee such an outcome. Even had they done so, there was still a sense of British difference and distance. Western European co-operation which, with Germany occupied, meant, in particular, relations between Britain and France, was actively pressed by the French as an option after World War Two. It also enjoyed backing from the Benelux countries. British willingness to offer support, however, was lessened by a suspicion of federalist intentions behind such co-operation. Furthermore, there was a strong determination to preserve independence of action, a determination that stemmed from a powerful sense of distinct identity and different concerns. There was intermittent interest, strong in particular moments, in the idea of a Western bloc, a term used in 1944-7 for West European co-operation, in a Western European 'Third Force', separate to the Soviet Union and the USA, and of a related military, financial and commercial 'Western Union' with France and other West European countries. Military considerations were most important in Ernest Bevin's 1948

'Western Union' concept (and economic co-operation focused on the Marshall Plan). Nevertheless, the British government and public saw the USA, the Commonwealth and the Empire, as more vital economic and political links for Britain.[1]

There was a hope that Britain could pick up the threads of its pre-war status. At the same time, it was believed possible to address domestic and imperial issues, such as social welfare in Britain and independence for India, without having to respond to international constraints, and, indeed, in a way that strengthened Britain. An independent India, for example, was seen as a continuing military asset. This general belief contributed to a sense that Britain was in a powerful position, and that it could benefit from the state of Western Europe, rather than needing to rely on developments there. However, this optimism was buffeted, and then overthrown, by a series of domestic and international crises. These were interrelated, particularly in the shape of Sterling crises and food availability. There was also a troubling series of international and imperial issues, including Soviet expansion in Europe and the Near East, and the status of Palestine. The development of the Cold War led to a dynamic that was outside Britain's control. This led, in 1947, to a reappraisal of Britain's position, and a stronger emphasis on Britain's need for alliance partners.

Thus, after World War Two, Britain's international position came to be seen very much as part of an alliance. In March 1950, Bevin declared in the Commons that 'the day when we, as Great Britain, can declare a policy independently of our allies, has gone'. Furthermore, compared to the 1900s and 1920s, foreign policy and defence came to play a central role in the concern of most peacetime ministries and took up a growing proportion of the time of prime ministers. This initially, however, did not lead to a focus on solutions within Continental Europe. Eastern Europe was occupied by Soviet forces and there was scant confidence that Western Europe could resist attack. Germany had been disarmed after defeat, with the eastern part occupied by the Soviets, and France and Italy seemed militarily weak, politically uncertain, and affected by Communist subversion. Spain was under Fascist rule.

Churchill, from 1945 to 1951 in opposition, but still influential, pressed the case for a 'United States of Europe' in 1946. However, he saw Britain as a friendly outsider, and stressed the need for a partnership between France and Germany (and not therefore Britain) as the basis for a new Europe. Churchill indeed declared, at a 'United Europe' rally on 14 May 1947, that the international order rested on four principal pillars: the USA, the Soviet Union, the British Empire and Commonwealth, and Europe 'with which Great Britain is profoundly blended'.

Ernest Bevin, Labour Foreign Secretary from 1945 to 1951, was similarly opposed to seeing Britain regarded simply, or even principally, as part of Europe, and wanted Britain to be treated differently from the rest of Europe in her acceptance of American Marshall Aid for post-war reconstruction. Committed to the continuation of the Empire, which indeed had proved a key military and economic resource for Britain during World War Two, Bevin, a firm anti-Communist from his trade union days, was also concerned about the expansion of Soviet power in Eastern Europe. Indeed, he helped to negotiate the establishment, in 1949, of the North Atlantic Treaty Organisation (NATO). This was both a necessary response to the threatening security situation, and recognition of the feebleness of the Western European response, one that remains instructive at a time of European determination to build up a separate military identity. Replacing the idea of a Western European 'Third Force', and in the absence of a European solution to the German question or to domestic British and Western European security issues, NATO reflected the willingness of the USA to avoid the temptations of isolation, but also the economic, political and military weakness of the Western European states in the face of Soviet strength.[2]

At the same time, there was concern, and not only on the left, that Anglo-American defence arrangements posed a problem. To some, they represented a loss of sovereignty, a point made in 1950 by Brendan Bracken, Conservative MP and manager of the *Financial Times*: 'What a wonderful thought it is that President Truman can ring a bell and give an order that

American aircraft can load their bombs and fly from London to Moscow! The interest of their visit will not be returned on Washington, it will be returned on poor old London. All this talk about giving up national sovereignty doesn't mean much when the President of the United States of America can use England as an aircraft carrier without the knowledge of the Ship's Company.'[3] Relations with the USA seemed the key issue to British commentators, not those with Western Europe. The latter was the site of these relations, but not their dominant shaper.

Within Britain, a sense of difference to Continental Europe was important. In part, this was a strong affirmation of a powerful distinctiveness, which had been heightened by survival in 1940, when the rest of Western Europe crumbled, by continued resistance thereafter and by eventual victory in World War Two. In part, a sense of difference was a matter of policy details. Defence proved a key issue, and the government was distrustful of French plans for a Western European army, the European Defence Community. These were seen by the French as a way to anchor Germany, and control its rearmament, a military equivalent in short to the plans for a coal and steel union, and a response to the need for a normalization of relations. British sensitivity to any sharing of interests and roles remained an issue, and politicians helped to affirm a sense of national difference. In 1950, Bevin replied to an American proposal by claiming that Great Britain was not part of Europe; she was not simply a Luxembourg. The people in this country were pinning their faith on a policy of defence built on a Commonwealth-USA basis – an English-speaking basis. People here were frankly doubtful of Europe. How could he [Bevin] go down to his constituency – Woolwich – which had been bombed by Germans in the war, and tell his constituents that the Germans would help them in a war against Russia.[4]

The same year, the Labour government had rejected an invitation to join negotiations for a European Coal and Steel Community (ECSC), finally agreed by the Treaty of Paris in April 1951, which was to be the direct precursor to the EEC,

with the same six members: France, West Germany, Italy, Belgium, Luxembourg and the Netherlands. This was a key moment, not least because the six pressed ahead to form the ECSC without British participation. The Labour Prime Minister, Clement Attlee, brought up the issue of the accountability of European institutions, a prescient point that remains relevant, but that had not hitherto played a major role in British discussion about European relations. He told the House of Commons, 'We on this side are not prepared to accept the principle that the most vital economic forces of the country should be handed over to an authority that is utterly undemocratic and is responsible to nobody.'

Accountability was related to the issue of national decision-making. Having nationalized these industries, Labour did not wish to transfer control to a predominantly non-Socialist, and certainly undemocratic, European organization, an instructive anticipation of the attitude outlined at Bruges by Mrs Thatcher in 1988, and one seemingly better understood today by Gordon Brown than Tony Blair. Indeed, Blair's lack of historical awareness is amply demonstrated by this issue. Coal had been nationalized in 1947, but iron and steel were not nationalized until 1951, and their presence in the public sector was seen as particularly important and contentious. Indeed, the Conservatives were to denationalize iron and steel in 1953. For France, in contrast, modernization of the economy required not nationalizations but planned co-operation with Germany in the key sectors of coal and steel.

When the Conservatives, under Winston Churchill, returned to power in October 1951, there was interest in strengthening Western European defence, but far less so in any new economic entity. Steel was to be privatized/denationalized by the Conservatives, not transferred to a European concern, and, again, British political assumptions came first, with no sense that anything else was appropriate. Although the British preferred the NATO solution, active support short of full membership was also provided to the European Defence Community (EDC), which was seen as a way to control a rearmed Germany, and the government only abandoned the

European Army concept in June 1954 when its failure seemed certain: passed by the other five Parliaments of the ECSC, the measure had proved bitterly divisive in France, and was rejected by the French National Assembly that August. In some respects, this prefigured the popular rejection of the EU constitution in 2005, although in 1954 the failure did not prevent the process that led to the creation of the, very different, EEC. Furthermore, in the 1950s, there was no willingness to seek support from a popular referendum. Had the EDC succeeded, it would have led to an important measure of political integration. This would have been led by defence, a field in which Britain played, and has continued to play, a major role, not the economic drive that was in the event crucial in the EEC.

In Britain (as in France and Portugal), there was still a strong commitment to Empire. Like its Labour predecessor, the Conservative government saw independence for India in 1947 as prefiguring not the end of Empire, but rather a continued international presence and identity based on its continuation, albeit more in the shape of informal control. In the 1950s, British troops were to be used to fight for Empire in Cyprus and Kenya, Malaya and Suez. Indeed, despite the commitment, through NATO, to the defence of Western Europe, which led to the continued presence of British forces in West Germany after the end of post-war occupation, much of the British defence effort was dominated by concern about imperial security and that of allies outside Europe. This remained the case until the late 1960s. A commitment to Empire was also the case with the French, also keen on establishing NATO and confirming American support, who devoted much military effort in the late 1940s and 1950s to trying to maintain their imperial position, first in Indochina and then in North Africa, a debilitating and unsuccessful project. The French, however, proved better than Britain at combining their imperial position with advancing their European interests, especially in the EEC.

British distance from the rest of Europe in part also rested on a cultural separation. In 1951, when the Conservative politician Selwyn Lloyd became Minister of State at the Foreign Office, he admitted that he disliked foreigners, did not speak any foreign language, and, except for World War Two, had never visited a foreign country. Lloyd went on to become Foreign Secretary in 1955-61. Holidays for many of those of Lloyd's interests were taken on Scottish grouse moors. This was an admission, despite Churchill's strong sense of identification with a united Europe, of what was a widespread lack of sympathy as part of a more general absence of cosmopolitan inclinations. If abroad meant the Empire (including the Dominions), it was an abroad understood in British terms. As Hugh Gaitskell showed, this was not only a Conservative position. It was also not an attitude simply of the 1950s. Nicholas Ridley noted that Margaret Thatcher, not a politician widely accused of cosmopolitanism, 'never attempted to speak in a foreign language', and she herself declared in January 1993 that 'the English language is soaked in values' that entailed political consequences. Ridley himself claimed that English was very different from both French and German, being 'very clear and unambiguous'.[5] Roy Jenkins was a prominent exception to this lack of cosmopolitanism.

There was a deeper reason, however, for distance. In Western Europe, many earlier political parties, especially those on the right, had been discredited by the events of the 1930s and 1940s, both Fascism and collaboration. These parties would be reborn in the form of Christian Democracy, a tradition very different from that of British Conservatism. Christian Democracy was more corporatist and more ostentatiously concerned with social welfare, and also looked to roots in a Catholic political activism that was very different to that of the Conservative Party. In Germany, Christian Democracy was stronger in Catholic than Protestant areas, and this remains the case. The movement for Western European unity indeed owed much to the growth of Christian Democratic parties,[6] and the institutions founded as a result reflected their norms. Although the links are unclear, and the influence uncertain, the Papacy consistently championed the movement.

In addition, across Europe, political structures had been found inadequate in the 1930s and 1940s. This created a situation of political and governmental fluidity, and led to a sense that change was necessary. The establishment of the EEC indeed was part of a process in which the political structures and party politics of France, Germany and Italy were transformed between 1945 and 1958. For West Germany, multilateralism offered a way to recreate an acceptable German identity and to bind it to the West.[7]

Britain was separate from this process of transformation. She also lacked the direct experience of invasion and devastation that all the founder members of the EEC had recently suffered, although many British cities had been heavily bombed. On the Continent, the disastrous experience of war, which, for France, was underlined by the serious post-war failures in Indochina and then Algeria, lent energy to the idea of European union, and not least to the willingness to surrender some of the powers and prerogatives of the nation-state to supranational bodies, in part in order to provide an institutional constraint on political extremism, of left or right, in any one country. Although the EEC helped protect democracy in the member states, especially Italy, there was indeed a deliberate democratic deficit built in as a structural part of the EEC, and this remains the case today, whatever the language of accountability. Such a process was easier for societies that were undergoing considerable centrally-driven change, and whose political structures were being similarly transformed, than it was for Britain; and this process also seemed less necessary for the latter. Similarly, although the role and nature of consent was very different, in Eastern Europe the destruction of earlier political structures in the war, the 'liberation' by the Red Army, and the subsequent establishment of Soviet hegemony and Communist rule, cleared the way for the economic bloc of Comecon (1949) and the security bloc of the Warsaw Pact (1955). Although they were far from similar to the EEC and NATO, there were instructive parallels. The Soviet Union tried to integrate the Eastern European economies, although it was handicapped by the inherent weaknesses of Communist economic management and also resisted by attempts by national governments, particularly that of Romania, to retain control.

Those states defeated in the war (Japan, Germany, France and Italy) experienced political and institutional change on the domestic and international level, while the victors (Britain, the USA and the USSR) essentially maintained their political structures. The changes that came in Britain were very much one-nation ones, for the Labour governments of 1945-51 were not greatly concerned to spread their model on the Continent. Indeed, British Socialist idealism was generally directed towards the Commonwealth, particularly India and the Empire, and focused on post-independence arrangements.

On 9 November 1954, Churchill, still Prime Minister, declared at the Lord Mayor's Banquet, that Britain was 'developing increasingly intimate ties with France, Germany, Italy, and the Low Countries which are stronger and more practical than any that have yet been devised'. However, in political and institutional terms, the establishment of the EEC in 1959, as a result of the Messina conferences of 1955 and 1956 and the Treaty of Rome of March 1957, was both effect and cause of a divergence between Britain and the leading Western European states; although it is mistaken to argue that French policy was driven by the consequences of the unsuccessful Anglo-French attack on Colonel Nasser of Egypt in 1956, particularly French anger with the British climb-down. Instead, French policy was already focused on the establishment of the EEC, and this was cemented by German willingness to accept the concessions France required. The six original members of the EEC were France, Italy, Belgium, Luxembourg, the Netherlands and West Germany. They were the Continental members of the European Defence Community.

The divergence between Britain and the EEC was taken further in 1959 when the British inspired a European Free Trade Association (EFTA) of countries not in the EEC, including Austria, Denmark, Norway, Portugal, Sweden and Switzerland. Subsequently, Britain was to make a free trade agreement with Ireland. EFTA was deliberately restricted to commercial matters, and lacked the idealistic and federalist flavour of the EEC: the Treaty of Rome had pledged to work for 'an ever closer union of the peoples of Europe'. Indeed, although essentially quiet, there is a distinct strand linking EFTA, and Britain's policy at the time, to attitudes that are still expressed today. EFTA did not represent opposition to Europe, but, instead, a different type of European identity, one rejected by the Six who formed the EEC. EFTA was established by a Conservative government, and reflected the degree to which British policymakers pressed for a form of European integration that matched their assumptions and was designed to serve British interests. The existence and goals of EFTA were a clear constraint on the possibility that the EEC would serve as the basis of a supranational Europe.

The sense of distance from the Continent was eroded in the late 1950s and, even more, early 1960s as Britain ceased to be an imperial power, a process that greatly speeded up from 1957. This was accompanied by a view that the Commonwealth, as most of the former Empire had become, would not be able to meet, or, indeed, contribute greatly to Britain's economic, political or security needs, a view that was to be fully justified by subsequent events. Support for joining the EEC became more widespread in British political circles, as it became clear that the organization would be more than a short-term flurry; indeed that it would be a success in terms of the level of economic growth enjoyed by the member states.

Western European growth rates were high, although this was not largely due to the EEC. In part, this reflected recovery from wartime damage, the sensible investment of American Marshall Aid and also the possibility of making rapid industrial advances by introducing American manufacturing and organization techniques. Structural reforms were also important. In agriculture, mechanization led to a movement of workers from the land, especially in France and Germany, into more productive sectors, and, therefore, to an increase in per capita productivity. Trade liberalization also helped greatly. The EEC took the credit for economic growth, although much in fact was due to the cutting of tariffs following the General Agreement on Tariffs and Trade (GATT) signed in 1947, a key aspect of the remaking of the world economic order in a more liberal direction by the USA, as American policymakers sought to avoid what they saw as a mistaken isolationism after World War One and, instead, to shape a strong non-Communist West. Similarly, NATO and, in particular, the American military commitment to Western Europe, was more important to peace within the latter, let alone its security, than anything provided by the EEC.

The Treaty of Rome lacked the utopianism seen with some earlier discussion of European federalism and, instead, focused on practical issues of economic transformation. The Treaty provided that tariffs within the EEC were to be removed within twelve to fifteen years; which in the end meant by 1968. Furthermore, the tariffs levied on imports from outside the EEC were to be harmonized at the average level in 1958. The fall, and then removal, of internal tariffs led to a rapid growth of trade within the EEC, one that excluded Britain from the benefits of their rising prosperity and therefore trade. This integration within the EEC created major problems of adaptation for producers, but it also brought major benefits. Growth enhanced profitability and encouraged investment, leading to fresh economic growth within the context of competitive pressures. In the first fifteen years of the EEC, Germany had an average annual growth rate of 5 per cent and overtook Britain as the strongest West European economy. France had an average annual growth rate of 5.5 per cent; Italian industrial exports also boomed; EFTA, in contrast, was a relative failure.

France had to dismantle a protectionist economic system in order to integrate, and, in return, it insisted that the EEC adopt an agricultural system that served its farming interests. To protect them from the effect of the free market, the Common Agricultural Policy (CAP) that, after hard negotiations, was finally agreed in 1962, provided both price guarantees and income support. This performed a vital political goal of reducing the rate of rural depopulation and easing social tensions. The CAP was an important aspect of the way in which France successfully pressed for a form of European integration designed to advance its own interests.

The size of its economy ensured that West German growth was particularly important. This growth owed much to

American aid and to growing global demand, but also to the economic liberalization, especially for foreign and domestic trade, pushed by Ludwig Erhard, who directed economic policy from 1948 to 1963 and was Federal Chancellor in 1963-6; and by other leaders, which was a major break from the cartels characteristic of earlier German history. Influenced by liberal-minded economists, the West German government adopted pro-competition policies and fostered currency stability, although, until it adopted the Godesberg Programme in 1959, the SPD opposition favoured state planning. More generally, the West German economic and financial system contrasted with the nationalizations and state control seen in France and Britain, let alone Communist East Germany, to which the West German concept of the social market was deliberately a rival model.[8] As Economics Minister, Erhard was sympathetic to the British idea of an International Free Trade Area (FTA), proposed in 1957, but Charles de Gaulle persuaded Konrad Adenauer, the West German Chancellor, to overrule Erhard and reject the proposal. The FTA answered British goals, not only in that the focus was on free trade, but also because Britain would have played an equal role in its formation, rather than having to join the already established EEC.

The loss of British influence in Washington was also an issue, as America was keen for Britain to join the EEC, an aspect of the long-term American strategy to move Britain from imperial power to the supporter of, indeed voice for, American interests in Europe. The British had earlier assumed that the USA would be happy to co-operate with Britain separately and closely, but this proved unfounded. 1959 saw the first bilateral meeting of American and Soviet leaders, showing that Britain could be left out. After the failure of the FTA, Harold Macmillan, the Conservative Prime Minister, applied to join the EEC in 1961, in part because he thought the Americans wanted a stronger Western Europe, as indeed they did. He feared that otherwise he would have less influence with the USA, and therefore be less able to win American support for British interests elsewhere in the world, and for the transformation of the British nuclear deterrent. Competition with France was also involved. Kennedy indeed pressed Macmillan to join the EEC because he feared that de Gaulle had ambitions to lead a Europe separate from American interests, and that the EEC might prove the basis for this Third Force.

Thus, a role in the EEC was seen as crucial to Britain's international influence.[9] This is an issue that has bedevilled British policy within Europe ever since. Successive Prime Ministers have been overly impressed by American views on the matter, but the logic to American policy is one that is destructive to British interests. Most famously, as represented by the oft-repeated remark about Europe lacking a single phone number, a comment associated with President Nixon's Secretary of State, Henry Kissinger, the thrust of the policy is for an end to national distinctiveness; indeed, a sort of tidying-up exercise. Furthermore, particularly in the 1950s, the USA was willing to encourage Franco-German reconciliation as an aspect of a necessary European self-reliance, although this was to harm British interests, and, in the end, to challenge those of the USA, especially, but even before, the Soviet threat had ended.

Macmillan's application to join was also linked to attempts at internal economic management. Having won the 1959 general election, in part as a result of a self-conscious consumerism deliberately fuelled by cuts in taxation and interest rates, Macmillan found by 1961 that the economy was hitting major problems, with a rising trade gap, higher wage costs, and an unsuccessful attempt to control wages. With the Conservative record for economic management under pressure, Macmillan, a corporatist who had called in the 1930s for state intervention, now showed support for government economic planning, which was presented as the way to ensure modernization. This was an important aspect of his rejection of the earlier policies of Conservative governments, seen also, for example, in his rush to part with Empire and also in his break with the Treasury team over public spending in 1958. In 1961, there was backing from Macmillan for French-style 'indicative' planning, and, indeed, France in the 1960s benefited from economic growth and restructuring, and from an ability to control inflation. In Britain, this aspiration led, in 1962, to the establishment of 'Neddy', the National Economic Development Council, with its task of creating a national economic plan, and its membership drawn from employers, trade unions and government. Macmillan's call for a 'New Approach', included not only more planning and better labour relations, but also entry into the EEC.[10] This was a response to the real and apparent weaknesses of the British economy, which the levels of growth existing within the EEC made more dramatic.

The entire policy failed, as government-driven approaches often do. The National Incomes Commission, which Macmillan saw as the arbitrator of incomes policy, was boycotted by the unions, Neddy had no real effect on policy, and, in June 1962, Charles de Gaulle, the French President, made it clear to Macmillan that he preferred an EEC without Britain, telling him that British entry would totally alter the character of the EEC in political as well as economic terms, and that Britain was too close to America. The last appeared underlined when Macmillan opted for American missiles as the way to deliver British nuclear warheads. In contrast, de Gaulle actively pursued reconciliation with West Germany, not least on his visit there in September 1962, leading to the Elysée Treaty between France and Germany in January 1963. Adenauer had moved towards de Gaulle and away from Britain and the USA in 1961, in part because he was concerned that the latter were insufficiently resolute over the future of Berlin, and other German issues with the Soviet Union. The link with France remained the alignment of German policy until Adenauer retired in 1963 and was replaced by Erhard. In return for the political weight Germany thus gained from French support, the German government was willing to make economic concessions to France,[11] and to accept the French verdict on Britain. This prefigured the closeness between the two powers in opposition to Britain during the Mitterrand-Kohl and Chirac-Schröder partnerships. As an instance of the role of contingency, once Erhard gained power in 1963, German policy then shifted towards Britain and the USA, hitting relations with France. Had this been the policy earlier, then de Gaulle would have been under greater pressure over the British application.

To de Gaulle, the nation-state, and therefore French interests within the EEC, came first, and this affected his policy towards the EEC and Britain. On 14 January 1963, notwithstanding the support for British entry from the other five members of the EEC, France vetoed the British application, de Gaulle declaring at a press conference at the Elysée Palace, 'England is insular…the nature and structure and economic context of England differs profoundly from those of the other states of the Continent.'[12] Britain would also have challenged French interest in developing EEC defence and foreign policies, and its shaping of the EEC's agricultural policy. With the Fouchet Plan, pushed from October 1961, de Gaulle envisaged a European Political Union, but, in practice, this French-dominated proposal rested on de Gaulle's relationship with Adenauer. British views would have been a hindrance. In the event, the Plan failed because of opposition from the Netherlands.[13]

A more general difference between the political cultures in the two countries had been demonstrated in October 1962, when Georges Pompidou, whom de Gaulle had appointed as Prime Minister that April, was immediately reappointed after his defeat on a motion of no-confidence in Parliament had led to his resignation. De Gaulle's attitude towards both Parliament and ministerial appointments reflected at once an autocratic manner that helped foster a democratic deficit, and a rejection of the political culture and structure of the Fourth Republic that was deliberately intended to achieve this goal. The Fifth Republic has never broken free from this legacy, but its ability to deliver the success it thought it could command proved limited.

The French veto dampened the debate within Britain. Although there was a degree of proto-Euro-scepticism in the Conservative Party, particularly among those who criticized Macmillan's views, it was Labour, then in opposition, that was more ambivalent about membership. In part, this reflected the traditional economic protectionism that had led to opposition in Britain to Free Trade in the 1900s, the grand 'project' for national and imperial renewal of the Edwardian age. In the case of the EEC, there was a fear that Continental workers would accept lower levels of social protection and welfare, and thus price their British counterparts out of work, an anxiety that prefigured French concerns in 2005 about the impact of EU enlargement, in the shape of Eastern European workers providing serious competition both by migrating to Western Europe and by producing cheaper goods in Eastern Europe.

There was also a sense of national identity under threat, memorably captured by Hugh Gaitskell, the Labour leader from 1955 to 1963, who declared, in a television interview on 21 September 1962, that entry into the EEC 'means the end of Britain as an independent nation; we become no more than Texas or California in the United States of Europe. It means the end of a thousand years of history'. Gaitskell's history was a bit dodgy: Britain had only existed as a state since 1707, and England had been conquered by Danes (1013-14) and Normans (1066) in the eleventh century, but he struck a note of Labour patriotism that had earlier affected figures such as Attlee and Bevin, and was to be seen anew with Benn. This contrasted with a Labour internationalist tradition that in some respects has emerged anew under Blair, albeit conspicuously not with the strand of international workers' solidarity. For Gaitskell, Second World War memories of the Commonwealth supporting Britain meant a lot. He declared that he would not sell 'the Commonwealth down the river' and that 'We, at least do not intend to forget Vimy Ridge and Gallipoli.' These were also memories that had meaning for Attlee and Bevin. Gaitskell too had been much affected by the unanimous hostility to British entry expressed at a meeting of Commonwealth Socialist leaders he had called in late 1962.

After Labour, under Harold Wilson (Gaitskell's successor from 1963), came to power as a result of the general election of October 1964, there was an attempt to maintain Britain as an independent power (while also using planning to transform the economy), which indicated a strong confidence in national remedies. Labour's policies, however, lacked a sound economic basis, not least because of an over-valued currency, acute balance-of-payments problems, and low industrial productivity, which were compounded by labour militancy and political mismanagement. These problems forced the government to abandon its political and military prospectus, and, in November 1967, in a humiliating fashion, its defence of Sterling, which was devalued by 14.3 per cent.

The failure of an independent strategy encouraged a focus on Europe, the despair remedy of the modernizers in recent British history. Discarding 'east of Suez' imperial commitments, defence priorities were focused on deterring a Soviet invasion of Western Europe. In May 1967, Wilson launched a new bid to join the EEC, securing a massive House of Commons' pro-entry vote of 488 to 62, although public opinion was not that clear-cut.[14] Having put entry into their 1966 election manifesto, the Conservative Party was in no position to complain, although many individual Conservatives did so. The populist nationalism that was to be offered and defined anew by Enoch Powell, when he began to attack the consequences of immigration in April 1968, was unacceptable to the Party leader, Edward Heath. Distrustful of Powell, and conspicuously lacking charisma or the ability to strike a patriotic note, Heath was no populist. Instead, he was to prove an ardent supporter of EEC membership. As such, Heath proved to be a poor definer and defender of national interests in opposition, just as he was to do so in government. In this, he prefigured Blair, although the latter was far more adroit as a populist.

Wilson said that political reasons were more important than commercial ones in his conversion to support for entry. Like Macmillan he was motivated by a sense of declining influence, not least due to the realization that bases east of Suez, particularly Aden and Singapore, could no longer be maintained. Wilson was also motivated by commercial considerations, not least the higher growth rates in the EEC. Unlike Gaitskell, he and the successive Foreign Secretaries, George Brown and Michael Stewart, were resolved on taking Britain 'into Europe'. Some of their colleagues, such as Roy Jenkins, later a pivotal figure in the EEC and, subsequently, an inspiration to Blair (pressing him hard, once Prime Minister, to adopt the Euro), were more enthusiastic about what they regarded as the political options and possibilities stemming from a greater British role within Europe. Like Heath, Jenkins scorned populism. His attitudes in social policy as Home Secretary reflected a contempt for majority views. Whatever the motive, there was more British political support for entry than there had been in 1961-3. De Gaulle, however, in November 1967, again blocked entry, this time emphasizing the underlying weakness of the British economy. A keen geopolitician, happy to think in terms of rival blocs, de Gaulle argued that Britain was driven to seek membership because of a sense of vulnerability, and, on 27 November 1967, he declared that the British people

> 'doubtless see more and more clearly that in face of the great movements which are now sweeping the world – the huge power of the United States, the growing power of the Soviet Union, the renascent power of the Continental countries of Europe, the newly emerging power of China – its own structures, its traditions, its activities and even its national character are from now on all at risk. This is brought home to her, day after day, by the grave economic, financial and currency problems with which she is currently contending. This is why she feels the profound need to find some sort of framework, even a European one if need be, which would enable her to safeguard her own identity, to play a leading role, and at the same time, to lighten some of her burden'.[15]

This geopolitical approach was to be rendered limited, if not anachronistic, by the flow of trade and capital. It also reflected a continent-based spatial imagination that downplayed the value of maritime links and oceanic identities, particularly the North Atlantic. As such, the approach was in line with the dominant historical strand in French strategic culture, one that was totally different to that of Britain.

In March 1966, de Gaulle had withdrawn France from NATO's integrated military command. This helped to create a major gap between France and Britain, as Britain made no such move to leave the military command, despite strains arising from Wilson's refusal to send troops to help the USA in Vietnam. As a reminder of the role of contingency in history, de Gaulle had failed to win an overall majority in the first round of the presidential elections held in December 1965, and was forced into a second-round run-off with Mitterrand in which he won only 55.2 per cent of the votes cast. In the first ballot of the French National Assembly elections held in March 1967, the Gaullists and their allies had won only 38.45 per cent of the vote. As another instance of electoral closeness, Labour won the 1964 election on 44.1 per cent of the vote, but the Conservatives still gained 43.4 per cent.

De Gaulle's rigid interpretation of French interests, and his unwillingness to compromise, helped ensure not only that Britain did not join the EEC, but also that it did not develop, either in terms of new members, or with reference to greater integration. Concerned that French interests might be subordinated as a result of the latter, de Gaulle indeed made clear his hostility to further integration. Instead, he proposed what was to prefigure later British aspirations: co-operation within a looser 'Europe of the Nations'. French obduracy led to the Luxembourg compromise of 1965, under which an effective veto existed for member states in many fields of EEC activity, and this continued to be the case until 1986.

Far from seeing de Gaulle's veto as an opportunity to concentrate on other issues, as John Major, for example, might have done once Prime Minister, the Wilson government responded by saying that it would not take 'non' for an answer, and, instead, that Britain would leave the application 'on the table'. Indeed, the government remained actively committed to negotiations, in particular seeking to maintain the support of France's partners, the 'friendly Five', so that when France changed her position, it would be possible for Britain to respond. The British position was helped when the Social Democrats, under Willy Brandt, came to power in Germany in

1969. The appointment by Wilson of Christopher Soames, a prominent pro-European Conservative, as British Ambassador to Paris in 1968, showed that, at least among the political leadership, there was now a consensus in favour of entry.

When negotiations resumed, there was a different President in France and a new Prime Minister in Britain. De Gaulle's resignation in 1969 after the French government had lost a referendum on constitutional changes, was a necessary prelude to the invitation by the EEC in 1970 to four applicants – Britain, Ireland, Denmark and Norway – to resume negotiations; Britain being the key negotiating partner. De Gaulle's successor, Georges Pompidou, President from 1969 until his early death in 1974, was concerned about growing German strength and the need to balance it, and not by the challenge from Anglo-American links. He was also more committed to the EEC than de Gaulle had been, and therefore more willing to respond to his partners' pressure for enlargement. By the time serious negotiations resumed, at the end of June 1970, Heath had replaced Wilson; the latter lost office on 18 June in a surprise general election result twelve days before the beginning of negotiations. The work done by the Wilson government, however, was important, not least because their official team, negotiating briefs and timetable, were all used by its successor.

Pushing hard for membership, seeing this as crucial to his vision for the modernization of Britain, Heath was also keen on a new geopolitical alignment. He was not eager for close co-operation with the USA, particularly under President Richard Nixon, whose policies had led to American intervention in Cambodia. Furthermore, Heath was determined not to be branded as the American spokesman in Europe. To Heath, Europe represented a welcome alternative to the USA. He was later to be hostile to Thatcher's focus on Anglo-American links.

Heath also saw membership as crucial to the revival of Britain's economic fortunes. Specifically, he regarded membership as likely to lead to an economic competition that would ensure reform and greater efficiency in Britain, prefiguring the view that Major was to take when pressing for joining the ERM even at a disadvantageous rate. In both cases, this was to be foolish economics and bad politics. Heath's views on the economic benefits of membership accorded with his emphasis on, and view of, modernization, the theme he pushed in the 1970 election campaign. However, joining the EEC would be far more disruptive for Britain than it was for the original member states, because their trade was overwhelmingly Eurocentric, while less than half of Britain's trade was within Europe.

As with Macmillan and Wilson, a lack of confidence in national solutions led to modernization being focused on the EEC. To Heath, Europe was the modern alternative to an anachronistic emphasis on global influence, and to a naïve confidence in the Commonwealth. Instead, he saw both prosperity and security as answered by European co-operation. The pooling of sovereignty and the creation of supra-national European institutions did not worry Heath, because he felt that a reformed and revitalized Britain would be able to play a major role in leading the EEC and shaping its policy. Indeed, Heath denied that the country would compromise its independence or sovereignty.

The negotiations were relatively easy for two reasons. First, Heath was prepared to surrender much in order to obtain membership. As a state seeking membership, Britain negotiated from weakness, but Heath seriously accentuated this, badly neglecting national interests. Although he had scant choice, Heath accepted the EEC's expensive, inefficient and protectionist Common Agricultural Policy, despite the fact that it had little to offer Britain. The CAP has ensured that the financial consequences of membership have repeatedly not served British interests. Indeed, Thatcher's obduracy over the Rebate was forced on her by Heath, who, characteristically, did not offer her any support over the issue. The resulting agricultural subsidies and higher food costs of the CAP replaced cheap food imports from the Commonwealth, particularly New Zealand lamb. They, indeed, had to be excluded to maintain the market for Continental products, while rising food prices fed through into the already serious problem of inflation. Entry into the EEC also led to a loss of national control over nearby fishing grounds, the sort of issue that characteristically meant little to Heath or to metropolitan opinion, but was of great importance to the fishing communities concerned.

Negotiations were successfully concluded in July 1971. Heath pushed membership hard on its economic merits, arguing that it opened up markets, and the White Paper claimed that Britain would be able to influence policy from being in the centre of Europe. In contrast, Heath said little about possible political consequences. He claimed in the Commons that there would be no lessening of 'national identity or an erosion of essential national sovereignty', and ignored warnings to the contrary. The extent to which this involved deception is one that remains unclear, but, at best, Heath was foolishly naïve over this matter, and the manner of British entry is a serious stain on his political record. It is instructive to compare his promises about the future relationship between Britain and the EEC with what occurred. As Noel Malcolm pointed out, it was just as well that Heath was not one's solicitor. Unfortunately, he could not be trusted with the conveyancing of the country.

Secondly, negotiations were relatively easy because there was only limited opposition within the Conservative Party, still less the government. The Commons voted in favour of entry by 356 to 244 on 28 October 1971. Heath had reluctantly conceded a free vote, the course urged by his Chief Whip, Francis Pym, in order to help win over Labour support, which was less than it had been under the Wilson government. Entry was criticized most strongly by the powerful left wing of the Labour Party.[16] This helped lead Wilson to declare that while he was unwilling to reject British entry in principle, he opposed entry on the terms which Heath had negotiated. Wilson was also opposed to the CAP, which he correctly saw as a serious burden for Britain. Labour supporters, led by Roy Jenkins, however, were willing to defy a three-line whip, and to vote with the government, thus providing a secure parliamentary majority, and one able to overcome both the bulk of the Labour Party and the role of any Conservative rebels. Although 39 Conservative MPs voted against, 69 Labour MPs were willing to defy their party and vote in favour, while 20 abstained. The Common Market Membership Treaty was signed in Brussels on 22 January 1972, and on 1 January 1973 it took effect, and Britain became a full member of the European Economic Community, the European Atomic Energy Community, and the European Coal and Steel Community. Denmark and Ireland joined on the same day, but Norway found the Common Fisheries Policy unacceptable. Large majorities against entry in public opinion polls in Britain were ignored. This was, more generally, a pattern in the politics of the period.

1 S. Greenwood, 'Ernest Bevin, France and "Western Union": August 1945-February 1946', *European History Quarterly*, 14 (1984), pp. 319-38.
2 J. Becker and F. Knipping (eds.), *Power in Europe? Great Britain, France, Italy and Germany in a Postwar World 1945-1950* (Berlin, 1986).
3 R. Cockett (ed.), *My Dear Max. The letters of Brendan Bracken to Lord Beaverbrook, 1925-1958* (London, 1990), p. 112.
4 R. Bullen and M.E. Pelly (eds.), *Documents on British Policy Overseas, series II, vol. 3: German Rearmament, 1950* (London, 1989), p. 4.
5 N. Ridley, *'My Style of Government': The Thatcher Years* (London, 1991), p. 159; Thatcher, 'The World at One', 20 January 1993.
6 D. Heater, *The Idea of European Unity* (Leicester, 1992), pp. 152-3.
7 R. J. Granieri, *The Ambivalent Alliance: Konrad Adenauer, the CDU/CSU, and the West, 1949-1966* (New York, 2003).
8 A. J. Nicholls, *Freedom with Responsibility. The Social Market Economy in Germany 1918-1963* (Oxford, 1994).
9 C. J. Bartlett, *British Foreign Policy in the Twentieth Century* (London, 1989), pp. 118-20.
10 A. Milward, *The Rise and Fall of a National Strategy, 1945-63* (London, 2002).
11 C. Wurm (ed.), *Western Europe and Germany. The Beginnings of European Integration 1945-1960* (Oxford, 1995).
12 A. Hoare, *Macmillan 1957-1986* (London, 1989), pp. 328-9, 446.
13 J. G. Giauque, *Grand Designs and Visions of Unity: The Atlantic Powers and the Reorganisation of Western Europe, 1955-1963* (Chapel Hill, 2002).
14 Anon., 'Public Opinion and the EEC', *Journal of Common Market Studies* 6, 3 (1967-8).

15 Quoted in R. Gibson, *Best of Enemies. Anglo-French Relations since the Norman Conquest* (2nd edn., Exeter, 2004), pp. 288-9.
16 L. J. Robins, *The Reluctant Party: Labour and the EEC* (Ormskirk, 1979).

CHAPTER 4

A VERY ROCKY MARRIAGE

EEC membership was re-examined after Labour returned to power under Wilson in February 1974, in large part in an effort to quieten critics on the Labour left. Far from displaying a principled commitment to a European cause, the divided government entered into a protracted and largely cosmetic renegotiation of Britain's terms of entry, which brought some regional aid and allowed the continued import of New Zealand butter and West Indian sugar. The fundamentals, however, were not altered. The 1972 European Communities Act, which gave EEC law primacy over British law, was not altered, the CAP was not reformed, insufficient thought was given to Britain's likely contribution level to the EEC budget, and the Commonwealth trading system was irreparably weakened. Although the government had hoped that it would be possible to bridge the Commonwealth and the EEC, not least by making the latter more 'outward-looking', British entry into the EEC was understandably seen by many Commonwealth members as a deliberate rejection of their interests; indeed, prior to entry, British trade with the Commonwealth was greater than that with Continental Europe.

Other factors, particularly the growing role of alternative sources of investment and markets, were also challenging this trade, but, nevertheless, the impact of entry into the EEC was striking. New Zealand agriculture was badly hit, with the number of sheep falling from about 60 million to about 55 million from the late-1960s to the mid-1970s. The percentage of New Zealand's exports going to Britain fell from 51 in 1961 to 6 in 1991, while, as those to Britain dropped, the percentage of Australian exports going to Asia rose from 49 in 1970 to 67 in 1991, and, in 1992, Canada joined the USA and Mexico in signing the North American free-trade agreement.

No real effort was made by Heath, Wilson or their successors to help the British fishing industry. Entry into the EEC led to a loss of national control over nearby fishing grounds, and contrasted with the extension of territorial limits to twelve miles in 1965. In 1976, the Fisheries Limits Act extended Britain's fisheries limit to 200 miles, but, under the terms of British membership, these fishing grounds had to be shared with other EEC states. The system of total allowable catches and quotas by species introduced in 1983 was designed to ensure 'equal access', a policy that hit Britain hard. Combined with the pressure on fish stocks, which was to lead the EU to impose far lower quotas on Britain in 1990 and 1996 under the Common Fisheries Policy, and with the sale of some fishing quotas by private interests, this was to help destroy much of the fishing industry. The pernicious nature of European justice for British interests was shown in 1991, when the European Court of Justice overruled the Merchant Shipping Act of 1988, which had been passed by the Conservative government in order to block the registration of Spanish-owned companies in Britain, in order to use British fishing quotas.

Although theoretically unrelated, British failure to defend fishing interests in the Cod Wars with Iceland (1958, 1973 and 1975-6) reflected a similar inability or unwillingness to sustain traditional positions. There was a major decline in fishing from once leading centres in the 1970s, including Aberdeen, Fleetwood and Hull, and fishing ceased at Grimsby in the late 1960s.

The renegotiated terms of EEC membership were passed in the Commons on 9 April 1975. Nevertheless, the governing Labour Party was far more opposed than the Conservatives, and the support of the latter was needed in order to get the measure through. 145 Labour MPs and 8 Conservatives voted against the Bill, and 137 Labour and 249 Conservatives in favour.

To surmount party divisions, Wilson then launched a constitutional novelty: a referendum campaign on Britain's

continued membership of the EEC. So that supporters and opponents could both campaign, the principle of collective Cabinet responsibility did not apply in the referendum. Held on 5 June 1975, 67.2 per cent of those who voted (about 65 per cent of the electorate) favoured membership, the only areas showing a majority against being the Shetlands and the Western Isles (of Scotland). The available evidence suggests that public opinion was very volatile on the EEC, implying a lack of interest and/or understanding, and that the voters tended to follow the advice of the party leaderships, all of which supported continued membership.

The opposition was stigmatized as extreme, although it was from across the political spectrum, from Enoch Powell on the nationalist right to Tony Benn on the left. Benn presented the EEC as an undemocratic 'capitalist club', and told the Labour Cabinet, of which he was a member, that 'on the EEC Commission, unlike the Council of Ministers, there is no British veto at all. You don't elect these people, they are Commissioners, and they are not accountable'. Benn also presented the EEC as incompatible with a truly Socialist Britain, not least by ending the possibility for national economic management. He argued that economic problems required the retention by the British government of power to introduce import surcharges, devalue the pound, and control capital movements, all of which would be threatened or lost if sovereignty was pooled within the EEC. Benn saw the size of the opposition vote as 'some achievement considering we had absolutely no real organization, no newspapers, nothing'.[1] This was scant consolation. The referendum result was decisive – Britain stayed in. Indeed, in 1993, a leading English historian, W. A. Speck, published a *Concise History of Britain 1707-1975* in which he claimed that his chronology 'spans the whole history of Britain in the precise sense', and explained that 'membership of the EEC was a partial surrender of British sovereignty'.[2]

Economic crisis in the mid-1970s, including high inflation, serious labour problems, and an inability to manage public finances, ensured that the Wilson and Callaghan governments were scarcely in a position to try to remould the EEC. Instead, there was a position of defeatism and a measure of despair. The need in 1976 to turn to the International Monetary Fund for assistance reflected the post-war failure of the British system, at least as it was operated in the mid-1970s. The Review of Overseas Representation (1977) by the Central Policy Review Staff, better known as the Think Tank, argued that economic strength was the basic determinant of power and influence and that, in light of Britain's relative economic decline, it was necessary to curtail her international commitments. As Britain's inability to maintain many of these became more apparent, the role of 'regional actor' seemed more tempting,[3] and this encouraged interest in the EEC.

As a consequence of the referendum, relations with the EEC were not to become as divisive a political issue again, until they emerged in the late 1980s as the focus for the ultimately fatal split within the Thatcher government. The anti-EEC movement itself largely disappeared from sight after 1975. There was no real controversy in 1979 when, fearful of the deflationary consequences of tying Sterling to a strong Deutschmark, the Labour government under Jim Callaghan decided not to join the Exchange Rate Mechanism (ERM), the only one of the nine EEC states not to do so. This was symptomatic of the reluctant Europeanism of the Callaghan government which, in turn, reflected Callaghan's ingrained Atlanticism. In light of subsequent developments, it is ironic that Margaret Thatcher, the Conservative leader, criticized the decision not to enter the ERM.

Under Thatcher, Conservative leader from 1975 to 1990, and Prime Minister from 1979 to 1990, EC (European Community) issues played no real role in the 1979, 1983 and 1987 general election campaigns; and it is possible to read accounts of them in which the EC scarcely appears.[4] In part because European integration did not gather pace, the anti-EC movement remained weak until it revived in the late 1980s. An instance of the complacency of this period is provided by Denis Healey's autobiography, which was published in 1989. He devoted very little space to the 1975 referendum, described

as an issue 'marginal to our real problems', which indeed were dominated by pressing fiscal and economic issues; while of the direct elections to the European Parliament, Healey remarked:

> 'Many of my colleagues feared that direct elections would give the so-called Euro-MPs the political authority to assume powers to override the British Parliament. In fact, as I predicted at the time, the Euro-MPs now have less influence on events than before. Elected by a small proportion of the electorate from very large constituencies, they lack political authority; and because they are cut off from their national parliaments they lack influence where it really matters.'[5]

Matters became more divisive in the late 1980s. Again this was linked to domestic divisions, although these had not been much in evidence earlier. This, indeed, was the case, for example, in 1984 when the rebate reducing the net amount of Britain's overall subsidy to the EC through the disproportionate payments Britain was making was introduced. A lack of acute domestic division was also the case when the Single European Act was signed in 1986. This Act was designed to give effect to the programme for an internal market launched the previous year. Such a policy of free trade seemed in accord with British views, and Thatcher had pressed for the opening of markets in order to encourage competition, but the increase in EC powers required to oversee the market was more of a problem in the long-term and should have been anticipated and guarded against. In enforcing open markets, the EC also proved open to political horse-trading that did not suit the British. Furthermore, the internal market was a major restriction of the role of individual states, and thus of the position and functions of government and Parliament. In addition, the Single European Market did not lead to the promised economic transformation. Furthermore, the Delors report on competitiveness and growth in fact aggravated structural economic problems.

Ironically, these years were to produce another major European 'project' that was to be a financial disaster, amply illustrating the contrast between aspiration and implementation that was to be more generally true of government-backed schemes for European integration. In 1987, the Channel Tunnel treaty was signed by Britain and France, and there was an initial public offering for Eurotunnel shares. In the event, as so often, the revenues were overstated, and the costs and risks unduly minimized. Construction costs in the event overran – by 80 per cent on capital costs and 140 per cent on financing costs. Operations began in 1994, but less than half the traffic forecast materialized, in part because low-cost airlines provided effective competition. As a consequence, by July 2005, share prices were less than 2 per cent of the peak value.

Keen on free trade, and an advocate for economic liberalization, Thatcher was critical of what she saw as a preference for economic controls and centralist planning in the EC. Both became more marked in the late 1980s as a major attempt was made to energize the EC. This attempt owed much to French Socialists, particularly Jacques Delors, and reflected their response to the problems of executing their policies within France itself earlier in the decade. During the Giscard d'Estaing presidency (1974-81), the conservative Barre government (1976-81) had pursued an economic liberalization, cutting the government's role and emphasizing market forces, that was in line with Thatcherite assumptions, not least in putting the control of inflation above the fight with unemployment; but these policies were dramatically reversed in 1981, after the Socialist candidate, François Mitterrand, won the presidential election. In many respects, the policies subsequently followed in France in 1981-3 linked the traditional nostrums of the left and of state control and intervention, with the aspirations for regulation and social management that underlie aspects of the modern European project. Reflation focused less on modernization than on support for traditional constituencies (coal, steel and shipbuilding in France in the early 1980s, agriculture today), while a determined attempt was made to control manufacturing and the financial system. Taxation in France in 1981-3 was directed toward redistribution, with a wealth tax matched by an increase in the minimum wage, and a cut in the working week.

This French experience was also anticipatory of current French and EU attitudes, in that it rested in part on a refusal to accept the disciplines posed by international economic competition, and, indeed, their rejection as alien Anglo-American concepts. Mitterrand's ambitious policies, however, had rapidly been thwarted by economic realities, and, to French politicians, Europe seemed not so much an alternative as a way to give effect to their visions. In 1985, Jacques Delors became President of the European Commission and he revived the policy of European integration, seeing it as a complement to the enlargement of the 'nine' to the 'twelve': Greece joined in 1981, and Spain and Portugal in 1986. To Delors, a stronger Commission and a weaker national veto were crucial if progress was to be made; indeed, he used the Commission to provide a driving force for integration, a position it lost in the early and mid-2000s as national governments came to play a more active role in the EU. The energy of the French left was strengthened in 1988 when Mitterrand was re-elected as President, while the victory of the right under Jacques Chirac in the National Assembly elections in 1986 was reversed in 1988 with the victory of the left under Michel Rocard. (Mitterrand remained president throughout.)

France's ambitions for the EC were accentuated when German unification became an option, as deeper European integration seemed a way to contain Germany, just as the original establishment of the EEC had been seen as a way to anchor West Germany. French ambitions for social policy helped ensure that Labour abandoned its position as an essentially anti-EC one and, instead, became the more pro-European of the two main British political parties.

Thatcher was very different to her predecessor, Heath, as party leader and bitter critic. Heath, who had been the chief negotiator in the application vetoed in 1963 and the key figure in securing entry in 1973, was, in turn, to be a bitter critic of her. Thatcher had no time for the integrationist ambitions pushed by Delors. She correctly discerned their serious implications for Britain and, indeed, Europe. In September 1988, Thatcher declared at the opening ceremony of the 39th academic year of the College of Europe in Bruges: 'We have not successfully rolled back the frontiers of the state in Britain, only to see them re-imposed at a European level, with a European super-state exercising a new dominance from Brussels.' Indeed, Thatcher could point to the economic revival of Britain as evidence for her argument that national rather than pan-European policies should be pursued. Membership of the EEC, in contrast, had not led to growth: British gross domestic product per person, which had fallen rapidly in the 1960s, continued to do so in the 1970s.

Thatcher felt closer to Ronald Reagan, the American President from 1981 to 1989, than to European leaders, such as Valéry Giscard d'Estaing, François Mitterrand and Helmut Kohl. Their patronizing manner was not suited to managing her assertiveness. Thatcher's government was also more influenced than its Continental counterparts by the emergence of neo-liberal, free-market economics in the 1980s, particularly in the USA. This influence reflected the greater hostility of much of the Conservative Party to the corporatist and regulatory state, certainly as compared with the attitude of the Continental Christian Democrats, let alone their Socialist counterparts. This situation was accentuated by the exigencies of coalition systems on the Continent, for systems of proportional representation are generally less subject to new political departures, or, at least, are so as a result of changes in which the electorate often play only a limited role. Kohl's Christian Democrats gained power in 1982 because the Free Democrats switched to them, whereas Thatcher had become Prime Minister in 1979 because voters' preferences had changed from supporting opposing political parties.

Thatcher's own attitude towards the EEC was more bluntly put by Nicholas Ridley, a minister close to her, who was forced to resign from the Cabinet after telling the editor of *The Spectator* in July 1990 that the European Community (EC, as the EEC had become) was a 'German racket designed to take over the whole of Europe'. Bernard Ingham, formerly Thatcher's press secretary, and, like Alistair Campbell for Blair, very much 'his master's voice', referred to the EC in 1992 as a

'Franco-German ramp'.⁶ Thatcher's alienation became more serious as the EC developed in a more ambitious direction. She was also unhappy about the unification of Germany in 1990, which followed the collapse of European Communism, fearing that this would lead to an overly-powerful and assertive Germany. Ironically, this mirrored earlier French doubts about West German *Ostpolitik*. To France, Germany had to be anchored in the EEC, to Britain in NATO, but unification made the latter a less potent context for German policymaking. German policymakers, such as Genscher, the Foreign Minister, claimed that unification would serve the interests of Europe, and the entire process was eventually put in a European framework; but Thatcher was uneasy about what this entailed. Genscher, indeed, was willing to exclude East Germany from NATO. The American administration, however, did not share Thatcher's doubts and, instead, actively supported unification.[7]

By signing the Single European Act, Thatcher had given new powers to the European Parliament and abolished the veto rights of a single state in some key areas of decision-making, but she no more realized what would flow from this, as the momentum for the creation of a single market gathered pace, than she understood the consequences of her failure to retain support among Conservative backbenchers. As a politician, Thatcher was gravely weakened by her inability to appreciate the potential strength of those she despised. She unfortunately failed to realize the possibility of holding a referendum, although she would have seen such a solution as a distraction from government policy and as an unnecessary limitation of parliamentary authority.

Thatcher had already fallen out with key members of her Cabinet, including former supporters, over what became the crucial issue of Europe. She fell out with the Foreign Secretary, the pro-European Geoffrey Howe, over joining the ERM of the European Monetary System, which constituted stage one of a projected economic and monetary union for the EEC. Thatcher was opposed because she saw the market as more benign than fixed exchange rates, and was also concerned about further European integration. Nevertheless, threats to resign by Howe and Nigel Lawson, the Chancellor of the Exchequer, led Thatcher, at a European summit in Madrid in June 1989, to promise to join the ERM. In July 1989, Howe was removed from the Foreign Office and made Deputy Prime Minister, but without being given power, which left him very bitter. The ambitious Howe was very much a statesman in his own mind. In practice, he shared Heath's lack of charisma. In October 1989, Lawson resigned, in large part because of disagreement with Thatcher over his support for shadowing the Deutschmark, which was an indirect form of membership of the ERM, and therefore unwelcome to the Prime Minister. He had done so in order to deal with fiscal indiscipline. Feeling weakened, Thatcher was reluctantly prevailed on to join the ERM on 5 October 1990, in part by John Major, the new Chancellor of the Exchequer, and by Douglas Hurd, the new Foreign Secretary, each of whom seriously failed to appreciate the possible political and economic costs. Labour fully supported the policy.

Thatcher, however, made it very clear that she had no intention of accepting further integration within the EC, not least a single currency. She correctly saw that monetary union was designed to lead to political union, a link Blair refused to accept. That path was clearly laid out by the meeting of EC leaders at the European Council in Rome in October 1990, which declared: 'The European Community will have a single currency which will be an expression of its unity and identity.' Thatcher firmly rejected this conclusion, and Britain was the sole state to vote against further economic and monetary union, sparking off the immediate crisis that led to her fall. Having resigned on 1 November 1990, in anger at Thatcher's clear-cut, indeed, strident opposition to further integration, Howe attacked her, in a speech in the Commons on 13 November, for being unable to accept debate and for her policy on Europe. He claimed that the latter was leading to Britain becoming isolated and ineffective. He also encouraged a leadership bid by Michael Heseltine, another supporter of the EC. Heseltine had left the Cabinet in 1986 over the Westland affair, when he had clashed with Thatcher over whether the Westland helicopter manufacturer should be taken over by an American company (as she wished) or by a European consortium, the goal he unsuccessfully sought. Having done insufficiently well against Heseltine on the first ballot, Thatcher, after initially resolving to fight on, stood down from the second ballot and resigned.

Economic links with the EC, meanwhile, had become closer. This was true of markets, suppliers, investment and regulation. The adoption of the Single European Act in 1986 committed Britain to remove all barriers to the creation of the Single European Market, and also altered the framework of British economic activity. The EC and the domestic market were legally joined, as it became necessary to comply with the Single European Market in order to operate in the EC and therefore in Britain. Tony Benn, by then a veteran left-wing Euro-sceptic, complained in 1991, 'Since we are in the Common Market, everything is international now. I mean there is not a single thing, including how fast you can go on to the motorway, that isn't a Common Market matter… You can get rid of John Major but you can't get rid of Jacques Delors.'[8]

As a member of the EC with, from the 1980s, thanks to Thatcherite reforms, less restrictive labour and financial conditions than elsewhere in Western Europe, Britain attracted considerable 'inward investment' from Japan, Korea, the USA and other states. Britain's relative economic decline had increased its already strong dependence on international economic circumstances, both interest rate policies and the inward flow of investment capital. Thatcher's appreciation of this helped to underline her general opposition to domestic and European fiscal and economic regulation. The results were clear. In 1991, 53 per cent of all Japanese direct investment in the EC came to Britain, creating tensions in Britain's relations with other EC states that reflected both a different openness to free market economics and the acute competition that the existence of the EC scarcely lessened. By April 1993, Japanese car-makers had invested £2.4 billion in Britain, transforming local economies and bringing jobs with factories such as the new

Nissan works near Sunderland; the chairman of the rival French car-maker Peugeot called Britain a 'Japanese aircraft carrier' ready to attack Continental markets. Nevertheless, in a deliberate move to lessen the role of the National Union of Miners, British and French national electricity grids were linked in the 1980s, leading the British power distribution system to become less dependent on electricity generated in Britain, and thus on British coal. Instead, French nuclear energy was tapped.

The political and fiscal relationship, however, was increasingly problematic. The Maastricht summit of European leaders, held in December 1991, brought a commitment to greater integration, which provoked opposition from within the Conservative parliamentary party. Although John Major, who succeeded Thatcher as Prime Minister in 1990, sought to distance himself from her confrontational style, and had initially spoken about his desire to place Britain 'at the heart of Europe', he still sought to defend national interests and resisted the concentration of decision-making within the EC at the level of supranational institutions. Furthermore, in the Maastricht conference of December 1991, Major obtained an opt-out clause from Stage Three of economic and monetary union, the single currency, and from the 'Social Chapter', which was held likely to increase social welfare and employment costs, to threaten the competitiveness and autonomy of British industry, and therefore not to be in Britain's competitive interest. Major also ensured that the word 'federal' was excluded from the Maastricht Treaty, although that was more a victory of style than substance.

The Best Future for Britain, the Conservative election manifesto for the 1992 general election, declared:

> 'Under the Conservatives, Britain has regained her rightful influence in the world. We have stood up for the values our country has always represented… We play a central part in world affairs… Britain is at the heart of Europe; a strong and respected partner. We have played a decisive part in the development of the Community over the past decade.'

Nevertheless, what was agreed at Maastricht was too much for the Euro-sceptics in the Conservative Party. The Treaty on European Union, signed at Maastricht on 7 February 1992, created the European Union (EU), the new term an indication of the new prospectus. Every citizen of an EC member state was to be a citizen of this Union, with certain rights in every EC country. The treaty also extended the scope and powers of the EC over its members, and announced that 'a common foreign and security policy is hereby established'. The scope of the EC's executive branch was extended over more areas of policy, including transport, education and social policy, the last a dangerously vague concept that threatened a progressive expansion of competence. In pursuit of 'a high degree of convergence of economic performance', member states were required to accept the fiscal discipline demanded by the Commission and the Council of Ministers. In addition, the ability of national ministers to exercise a veto on the Council of Ministers on behalf of national interests was restricted, while the powers of the European Parliament over legislation were extended. There were clear aspects of federalism in the division of powers between the EC and individual states. The criteria for convergence toward European Monetary Union (EMU) were also outlined, with an agreement that the national debt of participant countries should not exceed 60 per cent of GDP, and the budget deficit 3 per cent of GDP. These criteria, which were to be adopted for the Stability and Growth Pact agreed by finance ministers in 1996, were to be assessed in 1997 as a basis for EMU in 1999.

 The role of the Euro-sceptics was increased because the 1992 election left Major with only a small majority. This made it difficult for him to follow a policy on Europe that was not at risk from wrecking opposition. Euro-scepticism also provided a means for disaffected Thatcherites, angry at her fall, to express their fury, and ensured that the issue became a key one in steadily more bitter dividedness. The struggle to win parliamentary endorsement for Maastricht and the shape of the European Communities (Amendment) Bill badly weakened the government, which had to make it a vote of confidence.

In what Major referred to as 'gruesome trench warfare', the Conservative vote against the treaty eventually encompassed one fifth of the party's backbench MPs. The Paving Motion designed to take the Maastricht Bill through passed on 4 November 1992, but the vote was 319 to 316, a majority of only three. The treaty only became law on 20 July 1993.[9] The crisis led to the establishment of political groups that helped lead to the focusing of interest on the European issue. The United Kingdom Independence Party was founded in 1992 as a sequel to the Anti-Federalist League, and the European Foundation followed in 1993. This was not simply a development on the national level for, in 1992, the European Anti-Maastricht Alliance was established. However, European-level opposition to further integration proved difficult to arrange or apply.

Denmark, France and Ireland all held referenda on the treaty, but, aware of the unpopularity of its policy (and more generally of the government), the Major Cabinet refused to do so. This refusal lacked a constitutional basis as there had already been a referendum in 1975. It was also unpopular, ignoring a Maastricht Referendum Campaign that collected over half a million signatures for its Petition to Parliament. This was a major opportunity lost by the Conservative government and one that helped weaken its base, not least by dispiriting activists. The French and Irish referenda supported the treaty, but the Danes did so only on a second referendum, the first having led to a rejection, much to the encouragement of the British Euro-sceptics, and then to the acceptance of opt-outs on the Euro, judicial co-operation, European citizenship and joint defence in order to help win eventual consent. In hindsight, the failure to secure the British opt-out by a referendum was a major weakness, both in the short term and because it gave Blair opportunities for subsequent changes without having to face the verdict of referenda that would probably have led to defeats.

The government's reputation for economic management had already been crippled by another aspect of European policy. On 'Black Wednesday', 16 September 1992, an over-valued exchange rate, the interest-rate policies of the Bundesbank, and speculators, forced Sterling out of the European Exchange Rate Mechanism (ERM). Major had supported entry at what was an over-valued exchange rate because he believed that this would squeeze inflation out of the British economy and thus create an environment for growth. The government, however, found itself forced to respond to the financial policies of the strongest economy in the ERM, Germany, and was unable to persuade the Bundesbank to reduce its interest rates. The Bundesbank put the control of German inflation ahead of encouraging British economic growth, particularly given the inflationary pressures of German re-unification in 1990, and the resulting budget deficit. This incompatibility of two distinct nations' divergent interests demonstrated to British ministers the disadvantages of close international ties. The French government had similarly hoped that competition, once they joined the EEC, would squeeze inflation out of the economy, but they had been in a better position to influence German policy.

The ERM had been joined at the rate of DM2.95 to the pound, and this obliged the government to raise interest rates to defend the pound when its value reached the bottom of the permitted exchange-rate band at DM2.82. Indeed, it was fear of the deflationary consequences of tying Sterling to a strong Deutschmark that led the Callaghan government to decide not to join the ERM when it was established in 1979. As the ERM was seen as the basis for economic and monetary union, there was no willingness to accept a realignment of currencies. Having done great damage economically by joining, not least leading to a depression and an unsustainable deficit, the government felt that it had to stay in for political reasons, and the latter indeed had been crucial with Howe, Lawson and Major when they foolishly put pressure on Thatcher.

Departure was a humiliating defeat for fiscal policy, and one that involved the Bank of England in a futile effort to stay in, deploying over £15 billion from its reserves while interest rates were raised to 15 per cent. In practice, however, the exit brought crucial benefit, enabling Britain, in fiscal independence from the EC, to manage its own finances, and encouraging economic growth from the mid-1990s. In the 1990s, the British economy rose by an annual average of 2.3 per cent, which compared favourably to the leading ERM economies: 1.9 per cent for France and 1.3 per cent for Germany.

In a major article in the *European* of 8 October 1992, Thatcher wrote:

'This Conservative government, like its predecessors, should have as its main priority the maintenance of our constitutional freedoms, our democratic institutions, and the accountability of Parliament to the people… Thanks to the decision to float the pound, we now have a chance to follow an economic policy that puts British needs first… We now need an economic strategy which works with markets, not against them… We are warned, from home and abroad, that it would be a national humiliation if Britain were left in the "slow lane" while others sped towards economic and monetary union. But…a "two-tier" Europe, would at least enable the different groups of Europe to pursue different visions.'

At the time, however, the crisis created an abiding impression of inept leadership, and was therefore welcomed by Labour politicians such as Gordon Brown. Labour were able to direct attention from the extent to which, under the leadership of John Smith in 1992-4, it had backed the ERM and EMU. Indeed, the fiscal situation would probably have been worse had a Labour government been elected in 1992.

In a television address on 29 March 1993, President Mitterrand of France declared: 'Without a common monetary system, there is no Europe.' The ERM was the prelude to the European currency,[10] the Euro. Being outside it permitted Britain not only independent economic management, but also an attitude of 'wait and see' over the currency. Unacceptable to the Euro-sceptics, who wanted a commitment not to enter the currency, this at least ensured a reduction of tension over Europe in the last stage of the Major government. Nevertheless, that was only in relative terms, and the background had been a grim one. In November 1994, a Bill enabling an increase in the budget contribution to the EC that was opposed by Euro-sceptics, was made another matter of confidence by the Cabinet. This led to 9 MPs losing the whip, which cost the government its overall majority, although the whip was restored in April 1995. Euro-sceptics, however, played a key role in supporting John Redwood's unsuccessful challenge for the leadership later that year. From the other side, Heseltine, who then became Deputy Prime Minister, and Kenneth Clarke, the Chancellor of the Exchequer, took a more pro-European line, reducing Major's room for manoeuvre considerably, but without winning the government any popularity or giving it any impetus. Instead, their policies helped win support for the disruptive challenge mounted by the Referendum Party at the time of the next election.

These problems were exploited by Labour, and, indeed, helped encourage it in feeling that being pro-European was a way not only to define distance from the Conservatives, but also to do so in a way that would appear progressive. In part, this also stemmed from Blair's rejection of the Labour left.

In 1996, problems came from another direction when concern about BSE (bovine spongiform encephalopathy or 'mad cow disease') in Britain led to a ban by the EU on the export of British beef. The unwillingness of the EU to accept British assurances once the beef herd had been cleared, and a reasonable suspicion that this was motivated by self-interest, particularly on the part of France, greatly affected public debate in Britain. The crisis also led to a serious clash between the EU and the government, with Britain taking the symbolically potent step of not appearing at meetings of the Council of Ministers: the 'empty chair policy' that had been employed by the French in the early 1960s.

A sense of anger with the government led the Referendum Party, funded by James Goldsmith, to fight the 1997 election. One of the most prominent Euro-sceptic MPs, George Gardiner, who had been de-selected by his Reigate constituency, stood there for the new party, albeit unsuccessfully. By weakening the Conservatives, the Referendum Party helped Labour.[11]

The Referendum Party won no seats, but led Labour and the Conservatives to commit themselves to a referendum on entry into monetary union.

A brief narrative throws much light on the difficulties of the relationship,[12] but the issue can also be addressed in more analytical terms. It is necessary, in considering why the EEC, the EC and the EU successively failed to meet British interests, to look at the pressures placed on Britain's other international links. It is also important to consider the relationship with growing challenges to traditional patterns of identity, both the evolution of the British question – relations between parts of the British Isles; and shifts in British society so that the social underpinnings of deference linked to traditional assumptions about patriotism were first challenged and then overthrown.

Within Britain, there were also major shifts in the understanding of national identities. The increasingly multi-cultural nature of society and the impact of globalization, specifically of American cultural hegemony, had a major impact, but did not lead to any sense of affinity with Continental Europe. Within the UK, the tendency to blur England and Britain was heavily qualified, or, looked at differently, there was a greater understanding of different types of Britishness. British/English, British/Scottishness etc. were increasingly seen as very different. This encouraged a re-conceptualization of the multiple character of identity that left more room for adding a political view of Europe. This was eagerly accepted, however, only in Scotland and Wales, where Europe was seen by nationalists as a way to lessen the role of Britain. The 22 per cent of Scottish votes cast in the 1997 general election for the Scottish National Party was a comment on the decline of Britishness in Scotland.

Meanwhile, Britain's other major federal identity, as part of the Commonwealth, was eroding rapidly. It had been hoped that the Commonwealth would replace the Empire, rather than be a stage of dissolution, but in the 1970s and, even more, 1980s, it proved disunited, especially over British links with South Africa, and totally unable to meet earlier political hopes. Crucially, there was an absence of political and popular

enthusiasm for the Commonwealth within Britain (which matched a similar lack of enthusiasm elsewhere in the Commonwealth).

Meanwhile, cultural links with Continental Europe had grown and some distinctions between Britain and the Continent had lessened. The latter was particularly apparent in religious matters as British public culture ceased to be defined in Protestant terms. Indeed, in 1982, John Paul II became the first Pope to visit Britain. Travel also helped provide an experience of Continental Europe. Increased numbers travelled for pleasure, a consequence of greater disposable wealth, the development of the package holiday, the use of jet aircraft, and the spread of car ownership. If many who travelled to the Continent visited 'little Britains' in nondescript resorts such as Benidorm, others did not. The ownership of second homes on the Continent rose markedly, as did retirement properties. This was furthered first by the Channel Tunnel and then by budget airline services. Multiple annual visits became more common, but so also did visits to Florida. Furthermore, the opportunity of learning at least one foreign language was offered to all schoolchildren. On the other hand, university requirements for foreign languages from entrants in many subjects were abandoned, and comprehensive secondary education weakened language teaching.

The extent to which Britain was 'truly' part of Europe vexed commentators. In some respects, Britain and the societies of Western Europe became more similar, although this is also true of societies such as Australia and Canada, and, in part, the USA. This was a consequence of broadly similar social trends, including the move from the land and the emancipation of women. Sexual permissiveness, rising divorce rates, growing geographical mobility, the decline of traditional social distinctions, and the rise of youth culture were all shared characteristics, as was, with the exception of the USA, secularization. Social paternalism, patriarchal authority, respect for age and the nuclear family, and the stigma of illegitimacy, all declined in importance, while rights to divorce, abortion and contraception were established across most of Western Europe.

Populations also aged (although, again, not in the USA), decreasing the economically active percentage, and causing heavier pressures on the social welfare and health systems.

The relationship between changes in Britain's relations with the Continent and the European debate is suggestive, not clear-cut. Continental Europe became far less distant than was the case when entry into the EEC was first sought. This, however, was a matter of Europe, and not of the original EEC. Indeed, the enlargement of the EU is an aspect of this process, for the destinations being visited by tourists were outside the original EEC. This was more true of the Mediterranean accessions of the 1980s (Greece, Spain and Portugal) than of those of the 1990s: Austria, Finland and Sweden, all in 1995; Norway voted no for the second time in 1994.

Travel brought greater familiarity with Continental Europe, but only limited affection as far as politics were concerned. It was part of an explosion of consumerism that also took large numbers to Florida or Goa, a process that falling air fares to India, as a result of liberalization and competition in 2005, will take much further. Indeed, instead of encouraging affection, links with Continental Europe may lead to a sense of separateness. The anti-governmental ethos demonstrated by much of the population of Continental Europe is likely to affect travellers angered by strikes, while expatriates have been hit by policies of expropriation in Greece and Spain.

The democratization of the European experience for much of the British population, in large part as a result of travel, makes it much harder to be anti-European or xenophobic, but does not have any equivalent result in terms of relations with the European Union. This helps make the charge of being anti-European a far more effective rhetorical device for defining and discrediting Euro-scepticism, and it has indeed been used by Blair with considerable success, albeit in a characteristically highly dishonest fashion. Thatcher, indeed, was wrong-footed over the issue, and this was an aspect of the extent to which, towards the end of her premiership, she failed to grasp shifting political attitudes and assumptions. Unfortunately, these attitudes offered no guide as to how best to explain and advance

national interests in a context in which other governments were unwilling to accept British views. Blair was to suffer from this failure; indeed he was an expression of it.

1 T. Benn, *Against the Tide: Diaries 1973-76* (London, 1990), pp. 330, 384, 387.
2 W. A. Speck, *A Concise History of Britain 1707-1975* (Cambridge, 1993), p. 1.
3 J. Barber, 'Britain's Place in the World', *British Journal of International Studies*, 6 (1980), p. 106.
4 I. Crewe and M. Harrop (eds.), *Political Communications: The General Election Campaign of 1983* (Cambridge, 1986) and *Political Communications: The General Election Campaign of 1987* (Cambridge, 1989).
5 D. Healey, *The Time of My Life* (1989; 1990 edn.), pp. 458-9.
6 *Spectator*, 12 July 1990.
7 T. G. Ash, *In Europe's Name: Germany and the Divided Continent* (London, 1993); E. Pond, *Beyond the Wall. Germany's Road to Unification* (London, 1993); S. F. Szabo, *The Diplomacy of German Unification* (New York, 1993).
8 T. Benn, 'The Diary as Historical Source' and subsequent discussion, *Archives*, 21 (1993), pp. 8, 14.
9 D. Baker, A. Gamble and S. Ludlam, 'The parliamentary siege of Maastricht 1993: Conservative divisions and British ratification', *Parliamentary Affairs*, 47 (1994), pp. 37-60.
10 T. Padoa-Schioppa, *The Road to Monetary Union in Europe: The Emperor, the King and the Genies* (Oxford, 2000).
11 I. McAllister and D. Studlar, 'Conservative euroscepticism and the Referendum party in the 1997 British general election', *Party Politics*, 6 (2000), pp. 359-71.
12 See, more generally, H. Young, *This Blessed Plot: Britain and Europe from Churchill to Blair* (London, 1998).

CHAPTER 5

NEW LABOUR AND THE PROBLEM OF NATIONAL IDENTITY

The modernization strategy central to New Labour explicitly led to a remoulding of institutions, seen in particular with the creation of a Scottish Parliament and a Welsh Assembly, both elected in 1999, and with fundamental changes in the House of Lords the same year. The project for regional government was part of the same programme, one also in line with EU expectations as reflected in the creation, under the Maastricht Treaty, of the Committee of the Regions. However, this policy proved to be singularly unpopular with the electorate when it was consulted in the region thought most favourable, the North-East of England, in November 2004. Despite much government effort, 78 per cent of those who voted rejected the proposal. While this was emphatically not a referendum on the EU, it revealed large-scale popular disquiet about unnecessary change and regulation, and a willingness to dissent from a state-sponsored modernization project.

The sensitivity of levels of decision-making became more acute during the Blair years and more contentious. The establishment of a Scottish Parliament and a Welsh Assembly led to pressure for an English response. Labour favoured regional assemblies and not a body for England as a whole. Instead, in July 1999, it was the Conservative leader, William Hague, who suggested that when English matters came up for debate in the House of Commons, they should be debated only by English MPs.

As in the 1960s, modernization also led to an attempt to reconceptualize the nation, 'rebranding Britain', expressed in phrases such as 'New Country' and 'Cool Britannia', and seen with reference to the hopes placed on the new Millennium, and with the long-standing and finally successful ban on the hunting of foxes with hounds. On 27 October 1997, responding to this propaganda, the cover of *Time* magazine proclaimed 'Renewed Britannia'. Policy and aspiration, however, created a grave gap between government and people, as the reconceptualization failed to strike roots and, instead, seemed silly, while patriotism became even more contested territory than it usually is.

In part, these tensions focused on, and stemmed from, Britain's role in the EU. Labour's strategy of squaring the circle – making Britain central to the EU, remoulding the EU in Britain's shape, and solving trans-Atlantic differences – all rested on aspiration and hope. This strategy reflected a naïve misreading of the situation, rather than a sound grasp of the differing (and different) interests and views of other countries, the dynamic (or lack of dynamics) of the EU, and the likely impact of government policy on the British sense of identity. Much of this naïvety was expressed by Tony Blair, and, indeed, appears integral to his vision of the nature and impact of New Labour. He fell squarely into the Whiggish tradition of interventionism and the creation of systems to solve problems and prevent their recurrence, and was apt to underrate the pragmatic and prudential approach to foreign commitments. Because of the presidential system of power and policy during his administration (albeit with an autonomous and quarrelsome satrap, in the shape of Gordon Brown, at the Treasury), it is unclear how widely Blair's views are grounded (as opposed to just expressed) within the ranks of the government, let alone the Labour Party.

Although there is a general pattern in which Euro-enthusiasm had offered cultural and political visions reminiscent in some respects of earlier expectations about Empire and Commonwealth, much of this can be directly traced to Blair. His impatience with national continuity was indicated by his complaints about the weight of the past, alongside his espousal of a quest for the future. This was seen clearly in his comments about the need to break with a past of sectarian hostility in Northern Ireland, but also left a clear trace in the nature of the

Millennium celebrations. There was little attempt to look back, not least in terms of the contents of the Millennium Dome which included no section on history, and which, more generally, was a monument of banality. Although a handbook for immigrants prepared in 2004 under the auspices of the Home Office included 21 large-print pages on national history, the government decided that history should not form part of the citizenship tests introduced in 2005.

Under Blair, there was a frequent habit of apologizing for the national past, although this was a tendency shared with other Western powers. Blair's apologies would have been risible but for the present-mindedness it reflected. In 1997, he marked the commemoration of the 150th anniversary of the Great Famine in Ireland by issuing a statement declaring that those 'who governed in London at the time failed their people by standing by while a crop failure turned into a massive human tragedy'. This ahistorical admission of guilt was criticized by Unionists, committed to defending the historical legacy and memory of the Union, as well as by conservative commentators in Britain; the *Daily Telegraph* claiming that Blair had given support to 'the self-pitying nature of Irish nationalism'. In an interview in the *New Statesman*, published on 18 November 2003, Jack Straw, the Foreign Secretary, blamed British colonialism for many of the world's international disputes, again an overly simplistic account, but one nevertheless indicative of wider attitudes.

The government's attitude over Gibraltar was also symptomatic of an embarrassment over the national past, one that contrasted with Spain's robust maintenance of its Moroccan enclaves. The government, in negotiations with Spain, pushed the idea of joint sovereignty over Gibraltar, and Denis MacShane, the Minister for Europe, made it clear that this would not be prevented by a lack of consent there. However, the determination shown in a referendum in 2002 organized by the government of Gibraltar, in defiance of the British government, to remain British, rather than be party to any agreement to introduce a measure of Spanish control, struck a resonance in British domestic opinion.

More generally, in the early 2000s, there was a series of minor controversies, each indicative of the definition of a new post-imperial public history. There were calls by Ken Livingstone, the left-wing Mayor of London, to remove the statues of imperial generals, such as Havelock and Napier, from their plinths in London's Trafalgar Square; while, in 2004, a House of Commons' committee recommended the removal of imperial designations from the honours system, for example ending the title Member of the Order of the British Empire. Conversely, there were also complaints about a lack of state support for the new Museum of the Empire in Bristol.

A fundamental charge against New Labour is that it has no sense of the national interest. Indeed, the failure of the Tories to press home this charge, one that links foreign policy, defence, immigration, public culture and education, is one of the most significant signs of the crisis in Conservative politics and populism. Although allowance has to be made for a generally hostile media, nevertheless there seems to have been a central failure in policy presentation that reflects the Conservatives' difficulty in conceptualizing a clear and popular notion of patriotism within which perspective national interests can be discussed.

New Labour's lack of a sense of the national interest can be seen across much of the range of its policy and ideology. An aspect is the attempt to jettison much of the nation's past alongside a sense of distinctive national identity, and this is not unrelated to the European project of framing a history to match the manufactured constitution of the EU. A specific area of congruence is in regional policy. In emphasizing the regional dimension, which accords with the EU notion of the Europe of the regions, there is, in Britain, a downplaying of the extent to which there was a longstanding unity of England, which dates back to the tenth century. Furthermore, this emphasis on the regions is related closely to Labour policy towards Scotland, Wales and Northern Ireland; in particular to attempts to use devolution to end separatist pressures while, at the same time, keeping Wales and Scotland as major props to Labour's position in the Westminster Parliament. This entails a downplaying of the unionist dimensions of the histories of Scotland, Ireland and Wales, which indeed has occurred both in history and in 'heritage', with obvious consequences also for those of Britain and England. In 2002, the Scottish Parliament pressed for separate Scottish representation in EU institutions.

At the same time, mention of these different histories serves as a reminder of the controversial nature of identity and interest, and how past, present and future lie in a continuum in this respect. The charge against Blair and New Labour, however, is not so much that they have a different understanding of national identity and interest (and therefore national history), but rather that they lack a strong sense of either.

In the EU, there is a reiterated emphasis on what can be presented as European cosmopolitanism and, more particularly, signs of Franco-German co-operation. The former led to an emphasis on Erasmus, and the latter to the celebration of more obscure individuals. In 1994, I was invited (all costs paid) to Strasbourg for a conference on Jean-Daniel Schoepflin, a key Alsatian intellectual of the eighteenth century who was celebrated as a sympathetic figure linking France and Germany. (I particularly enjoyed the conference meals.) The emphasis on Schoepflin was an attempt to link the EU, presented in terms of the progressive cause of European reconciliation, with those politicians and intellectuals who supported the Franco-Austrian alignment of 1756-91. This argument fulfilled several purposes. It suggested that hostility between France and the Germanic world was an anomaly and blamed this in part on the role of Frederick the Great of Prussia. Thus, German nationalism could be seen as a false consciousness because it was constructed by Prussia, while, in contrast, a true German nationalism rested on co-operation with France. The Catholic and Enlightenment aspects of this argument could also be stressed.[1] Unfortunately, this argument underplayed the marked unpopularity of the Austrian alignment within France, and the extent to which conflict with Austria was a much stronger theme from 1673 to 1860.[2] Indeed, prefiguring present debates, foreign policy raised the issue of the legitimacy of public opinion as opposed to government views.[3]

In the EU, there has also been a presentation of the Frankish invaders of Gaul in terms of a synthesis of Germany and France, rather than a violent and disruptive discontinuity. This led to an emphasis on Clovis and, even more, Charlemagne. The latter, prefiguring French presentations of Napoleon, was seen as anchoring the Franks within a wider concept of Christendom. This was not, however, a presentation that would have meant much to the Lombards or Saxons, both of whom suffered greatly at his hands. A concept of Europe focused on Charlemagne also excluded Britain and Eastern Europe, particularly the Eastern Roman (Byzantine) Empire. Reference to Charlemagne ironically linked the EU to Vichy, which had also used him as a symbol.

The EU's history is Continental and inward-looking, one that offers little to Europe's Atlantic heritage which is particularly strong in the case of Britain. At the start of a new Millennium, it is all too easy to forget that what made Europe, and most especially Britain, distinctive in world history was its ability to use the oceans in order to create the first trading systems and empires able to span the world. Easy to forget in part because of the nature of Europe now, but also because of the way in which European identity is currently understood. Now, Europe's attitude towards the outside world is at once vainglorious and defeatist. There has been repeated talk of the EU, the Euro and European foreign policy initiatives as being able to rival the USA, but also an awareness that they have been unable to do so. Indeed, the Bosnian crisis and that in Kosovo made it clear that European states and federal institutions were only able to address issues of Balkan stability by turning to the USA for support. Blair took a particularly active role in engaging Clinton's commitment to the Kosovo issue. Some Europeans are clearly unhappy about the strength of American power – military, political, economic and cultural – a situation that was exposed and accentuated in 2002-3, during the debate over policy towards Iraq; although the roots of difference went far deeper, and were related, in particular, to an ambivalence about change and an uneasiness with the impression of European powerlessness in the face of American strength.

The EU represents a view of Europe not only today and for the future, but also for the past. This view is one that sees European identity as central to the real interests and histories of European peoples and countries, and this encourages an emphasis on links within Europe, a process that has gained strength with the fall of the Iron Curtain in 1989-91, and the subsequent attempt to incorporate Eastern Europe into the political, economic and military structures of Western Europe. The attempt has a clear cultural correlate, as it seeks to persuade the peoples of Western Europe that their prime identity is as Europeans, and that their countries have a European character and destiny; Europe being seen as much more than a matter of geography.

To modern readers, this may seem a matter of stating the obvious, but primarily owing to two factors, this is far from the case. Firstly, for much of the last 600 years, a large part of Eastern Europe has been part of a very different cultural (and political) world, that of the Ottoman (Turkish) Empire, an Islamic imperial state with its capital at Constantinople (Istanbul) that spent much of the period in conflict with Christian powers, and whose geographical scope included much of the Middle East and North Africa. Turkey's heritage thus stretches to Basra, Mecca and Algiers. Although modern scholarship can search for parallels between (Christian) European governments and societies, and those of the Ottoman Empire, to contemporaries the empire was not so much non-European as anti-European. It defined that which was not European, both tyranny and Islam, and presented both as a threat, understandably so when Turkish armies twice advanced to Vienna. There is a clear historical background to modern cultural rejection of a concept of Europe that includes modern Turkey. Nevertheless, in December 2004, Jack Straw felt able to declare that, 'Turkey is an essentially European country', an assertion characteristically not supported by any evidence and one that, as a result, sits alongside contrary assertions such as those of Fritz Bolkestein, an EU Commissioner critical of Turkish accession. In September 2004, he compared the large-scale immigration from Turkey

that he predicted, with reason, would follow accession with past political challenges from the Ottoman Empire, declaring 'the liberation of Vienna in 1683 will have been in vain'. More relevant historical discussion focuses on the nature of Turkish development in the twentieth century. The latter has been particularly contentious in the case of Turkish unwillingness to confront the Armenian massacres of the 1910s, while there has also been European criticism of the authoritarian nature of Atatürk's regime. In contrast, within Turkey, there is scant criticism of the foundation figure of modern Turkey. Prominent supporters of Turkish entry into the EU include Blair and Chirac.

Secondly, if 'Europe' did not extend into the Ottoman world, it did spread across the oceans. The great expansion changed the world, but it also altered Europe. This was true both of the Europe from which trade, territorial control and colonizers came, and the rest of Europe which was affected by the expansion, for example through the provision of transoceanic goods, such as sugar and tea, as well as, directly or indirectly, by shifts in advantage and interest stemming from these changes. By 1750, as a result both of Ottoman conquests and of the great European expansion, London, Paris, Lisbon and Madrid had more in common with colonial centres, such as Philadelphia, Québec, Rio and Havana, than they did with cities under Ottoman rule, such as Belgrade, Bucharest and Sofia. Furthermore, this situation remained the case over the following century, even as the bulk of the American empires of the European powers gained independence. With a different geography, this pattern of similarity and contrast was to resume during the Cold War.

It is this tradition that is questioned directly by the creation of a new European history, for, alongside the challenge to the individual states of the EU that has attracted most attention, and caused particular controversy in Britain, has come a determination to marginalize the residue and influence of empire, so that past links are treated as anachronistic, if not undesirable. These processes influence both present policy and cultural formation: in the case of the former, there has been the successful downplaying of economic links with former colonies, a shift highlighted by the fate of New Zealand lamb imports to Britain in the 1970s, once the agricultural protectionism of the EEC had been implemented, and by Britain's difficulties in retaining preferential terms for banana imports from its former West Indies colonies.

Issues of definition are made complex by the range of possible criteria. Europe can be treated geographically, although once more precision is sought than the statement that it is located between Asia and the Atlantic, such a treatment is open to debate. The Urals, for example, are neither a barrier nor a frontier. Europe can also be treated as a value system, a goal or an ideology. The EU has been successful in presenting itself as the means, indeed goal, of public myths of European identity. This can be seen in terms of the language used by British politicians and commentators. Politicians talked in the 1960s and 1970s of 'entering Europe', and, in the 1980s, Thatcher's views led to her being presented as 'anti-European', although she saw herself as opposed to Euro-federalism. Indeed, Thatcher was more concerned about the situation in Eastern Europe than the Euro-federalists.

National history indeed proved controversial during the Blair years, as seen with the furore associated with Norman Davies' best-selling national history, *The Isles: A History* (1999). The *Times* was in no doubt of what it had bought: on 1 November 1999, the Features section of the newspaper began a serialization of excerpts from the work heralded with: 'In the most controversial history book of the decade, Norman Davies traces the story of our islands... He finds that much of the history we have been taught is untrue.' The Features section included a piece by Davies stating: 'It would be hard to find another country that is so befuddled about its past.' The newspaper's leader that day proclaimed: 'A history which rescues our past from anachronism... It effortlessly supersedes the attempt of journalists and generalists to lend coherence to the national narrative... History is presented in all its complexity', and so on. There is no suggestion in what Davies wrote, of limitations or debate, and apparently no alternative, to the 'microscopes' of academic specialism and the flaws of the ignorant generalist, bar Davies.

In the *Daily Mail*, however, four days later, Andrew Roberts, a conservative columnist and popular historian, began: 'This is a dangerous book, written at a dangerous time', a reference to New Labour's assault on the role of history in British culture. Later in his piece, Roberts claimed: 'Because this book is so unrelentingly critical of so many aspects of British institutions and "Old Britain" – especially the Monarchy – it has been hailed in *bien pensant* New Labour circles as intellectual justification for their ideological preconceptions in favour of devolution, regionalism and pooling British sovereignty through closer European integration.' Roberts, who saw Davies' book as an assault on 'the legitimacy of the British nation state', wrote: 'With willpower and self-confidence, the present threats can be overcome... United we stand, Daviesed we fall.'

On 23 December 1999, Nigel Jones followed up by launching a strong attack on Davies in the *Times*:

> 'It is no coincidence that this determined attempt to airbrush England and Englishness out of the historical narrative comes at precisely the moment when the Government should be actively seeking to subsume our age-old national identity in a remote, centrally-directed, unelected, inorganic foreign body...our own "cultural cringe": the idea that continental Europe is, by definition, a superior entity, that all roads lead to and from Rome; and that European notions, whether pronounced by Popes, by despot monarchs, by committees of public safety and Nuremberg rallies, or promulgated by philosophers from Rousseau to Marx to Nietzsche, are, *ipso facto*, the bee's knees. This is the self-hating England exemplified by James I, Charles I and James II, Harley and Charles James Fox, Philby *père et fils*, Lytton Strachey and Sir Oswald Mosley; and in our day, by the likes of Edward Heath, Hugo Young, Ken Clarke and Chris Patten... As a leading light in what might be called the "collaborationist" school

of historians, Davies deplores each and every event that gave these islands their unique distinctiveness – from the continental shift that let in the Channel...down to the Reformation.'

Jones' historical resonance was briefly reprised by Bill Cash in the House of Commons on 9 February 2005, when unsuccessfully tabling amendments to the European Union Bill: 'The fundamental question is one of political will. Who governs this country? People have fought and died over that question.' To Cash, the rejection of James II and VII in 1688-9 was an assertion of parliamentary rule while the Treaty on European Union was a prerogative act, made clear by the argument of Jack Straw that international treaties took precedence over national laws; and, as Straw told the European Scrutiny Committee on 8 February 2005, that even if the treaty was rejected in a referendum, the government would not repeal the resulting legislation.

Aside from Davies, also in 1999, there had come an explicit official call for a rewriting of history. The Commission on the Future of Multi-Ethnic Britain declared that, 'Britishness as much as Englishness, has systematic, largely unspoken, racial connotations', and called for a change in historical treatments, specifically 'reimagining' to challenge racism. This was linked to Euro-scepticism by Denis MacShane, the highly europhile Minister for Europe, who, in an interview published in the *Daily Telegraph* on 7 August 2004, declared: 'We have got a dark streak of xenophobia and racism in our mentality and our nature. Anti-Europeanism allows it to get a lot closer to the surface... Euroscepticism is a misnomer. What we are talking about is a hatred of Europe.' With ministers like that, it was scarcely surprising that the government found it difficult to articulate a patriotic sense of national interest.

As David Willetts pointed out in October 2004, the Blair government had drawn on the ideas of a number of historians who emphasized the extent to which nations were imagined communities. He named Linda Colley, who had indeed made a presentation for Blair, David Cannadine, who had links to Gordon Brown, Eric Hobsbawn and Perry Anderson. Earlier, Michael Gove had also criticized Cannadine and Colley.[4]

Blair's willingness to advocate major changes in domestic government that amounted to a cultural shift ensured that his approach to Europe was dissimilar to that generally followed hitherto. Successive governments had sought a pragmatic, step-by-step approach to European co-operation on 'unwritten lines'; while the Continental course was for blueprints, intellectual clarity and comprehensiveness expressed in constitutional form. This contrast was made by Ernest Bevin in a speech on 'Western Union' on 22 January 1947, when he advocated what he termed a 'practical programme', rather than 'ambitious schemes'. Although he liked to see himself as practical, Blair very much broke from this model. Indeed, there was a serious gap, in both foreign and domestic policy, between Blair's willingness to propose bold solutions and his repeated failures in implementation.

Blair took office in 1997 intent on mending relations in Europe,[5] at once a critique of the Tories and an offer of a new beginning. He had promised that a Labour government would be a constructive partner, but would not abandon national interests. However much his concept of an ethical foreign policy was novel, the Foreign Office Mission Statement launched by the new Foreign Secretary, Robin Cook, embodied the traditional British view of Europe. Britain hoped to play a leading role in a Europe of independent nation-states.

More sympathetic to the European ideal than his predecessors since Heath's fall in 1974, Blair was convinced that closer European integration was central to his strategy for modernization. The opt-out from the Social Chapter was relinquished in 1997, leading to more regulations for employers. Attention focused on the single currency, the Euro, as the EU moved towards establishing it. Blair felt that its adoption would strengthen Britain's political position in Europe. At that stage, the new Chancellor of the Exchequer, Gordon Brown, also had a commitment to the Euro, and in a speech delivered at Chatham House on 17 July 1997 he declared that, 'In order to shape an agenda that is right for Britain and Europe we need to be in and leading in Europe.'

Nevertheless, speculation on what such remarks meant in terms of the Euro became insistent. In a Commons' statement on 27 October 1997, Brown stated that there were no constitutional reasons why Britain should not join the single currency, although, as short-term interest rates then were nearly 4 per cent higher in Britain than in Germany or France, he judged the economic case as not then favourable. Brown declared that 'British membership of the single currency in 1999 could not meet the tests' and 'there is no realistic prospect of our having demonstrated before the end of this parliament that we have achieved convergence that is sustainable and settled rather than transitory'. Brown was to be put under considerable pressure by Blair to fudge the economic tests for membership of the Euro, but he rejected it. Against Blair's wishes, the Treasury was allowed to make an objective assessment, which was negative,[6] although concerns remained that the judgments of the degree of convergence and flexibility were arbitrary and therefore could be influenced by political decisions.

The fate of the Euro at this stage was unclear, but in November 1998 the simultaneous Eurozone interest rate cut, by what were eleven still-autonomous central banks, suggested that it would work. On 23 February 1999, a government-sponsored national changeover plan to ease the introduction of the single currency was introduced. This step, declared Blair, showed that his government had 'changed gear' in its approach towards the single currency. The Trades Union Congress was enthusiastic about joining, but the government did badly in the 1999 European elections, suggesting that a referendum would be very damaging. The following year, William Hague, the Conservative leader who had succeeded Major, launched a 'Save the Pound campaign'. The Euro had already energized a range of opposition including Business for Sterling and New Europe, both founded in 1998: they combined to form No in 1999, paving the way for a referendum battle. These organizations were joined by the British Democracy Campaign in 2001 and Labour Against the Euro in 2002.

Britain did not join the Euro when it was launched as a trading currency on 1 January 1999; notes and coins followed in 2002. Blair felt obliged to be cautious because of the degree of scepticism among the public, not least the popular press; and because the economy was on a different cycle from the rest of the EU, a situation that reflected very different fundamentals. The problems of the Euro were also an issue. A sharp initial fall in its value was followed in the autumn of 2000 by another major fall, while in 2001, the European Central Bank's failure to lower interest rates was blamed both for the recession across much of the Eurozone and for problems with the world trading system.

Conservative pressure against the Euro was also a factor in Blair's caution. In order to draw the sting of the Conservative 'Keep the Pound' campaign in the 2001 election, Labour promised a referendum on the issue, one that entailed delay until such a time when Blair thought that it could be readily won. The Euro was rejected in referenda in Denmark in 2000 and in Sweden in 2003. The Swedish vote was particularly instructive for British pundits. On a high turnout of 81.2 per cent, 56.1 per cent voted against adopting the Euro. This was despite the support for adoption by all the major parties and newspapers and the shock caused by the unrelated murder of the pro-Euro Foreign Minister, Anna Lindh. The Swedish vote influenced the politics of British entry, just as the fact that Britain had not joined affected the Swedes.

At the same time, in 2002, the imperial measures were lost. The 1985 Weights and Measures Act, passed during the Thatcher years, had established the right to use such measures, but the primacy of the European Communities Act was such that, in 2002, EU regulations were stated to be the valid ones, and the 'Metric Martyrs' lost their case.

The linkage between the Euro and the Blair-Brown relationship was not restricted to the late 1990s, although the situation in the early and mid-2000s remains obscure. It has, nevertheless, been claimed that, in 2001-2, Blair offered to retire as Prime Minister if the Treasury would back the Euro, but that Brown rejected this on the grounds that joining the

Euro would ensure Labour unpopularity and would therefore lead to defeat in the next election.[7] Brown understood not only the details of the Euro, as Blair failed to do, but also appreciated the political dangers the EU posed. Indeed, this led him to press Blair to agree that the European constitution could only be adopted after a referendum, a measure that greatly restricted Blair's freedom of manoeuvre.

Despite Blair's claims about being able to be more influential in Europe than the Conservative governments had been, the direction of EU policy owed little to his views. The left-wing governments elected in France and Germany in 1997-8, headed by Jospin (Prime Minister, not the President, who was still Chirac) and Schröder respectively, had scant sympathy for Blair's determination to move Labour away from Socialism. Just as Thatcher had been concerned that changes within Britain would be reversed at the European level, so Blair rapidly acquired the same concern, although, unlike Thatcher, he hoped to be able to change European minds. In particular, it seemed apparent that the modernization project that Blair championed, and his desire to revive the economy by following pro-business policies, were threatened by the policies and attitudes of European institutions and the dominant Franco-German axis.

The irrelevance of British views was particularly seen in 2002, when France and Germany reached a bilateral agreement over the future of farm support payments, which then became the basis of EU policy. This was a policy that Blair reluctantly agreed to, displaying his weakness in EU politics. Under this agreement, the Common Agricultural Policy (CAP) was to remain unchanged until 2012, despite the pressure on EU budgets and the likely consequences of Eastern European accession. Much of the resulting burden will be borne by Germany.

The CAP is a system that has much helped French farmers. Designed to prevent structural changes in response to international competition, this policy ensured that the expenditure of the EU was particularly not in Britain's interest (a situation improved, but not ended, by the British rebate). In 2001,

France received 22 per cent of CAP subsidies (Spain, Greece and Ireland were the other major beneficiaries), and since 1994 French farmers have received £68.6 billion. Far from preserving a French way of life, however, subsidies bolstered the already most prosperous and productive sections of French agriculture, particularly the large cereal producers of the prairies of the Île-de-France, and the intensive poultry and pork farmers of the west. In effect, a guaranteed market and certainty in high prices provided the security for mechanization and the large-scale use of chemical fertilizers. Politically, this constituency helped provide voting and financial support for major interests.

Despite this support, however, much of French agriculture proved uncompetitive. Indeed, there was a disjuncture between the heavily-subsidized, large-scale French agri-businesses that crucially competed with the USA in world markets for agricultural imports, and small-scale producers who increasingly went bankrupt in the face of over-production. The role of the farmer nevertheless remained important, even though the number of farms in France fell from about 1.6 million in 1970 to about 700,000 in 2005. Chirac, a former Minister of Agriculture, very much identifies with his rural constituency in the Corrèze and has presented the countryside in terms of an immutable Frenchness. The CAP led to large-scale fraud (notoriously so in Italy), to a higher cost for food, to problems in international trade, and to the moral problem outlined in the World Development Bank Human Development Report of 2003, which suggested that each EU cow was the subject of $913 of annual subsidies, a sum considerably greater than that spent on overseas relief to those suffering dearth and malnutrition.

In contrast, the relatively small size of the agricultural sector in Britain ensured that it was of only modest importance as a source of income or employment; while the long-term consolidation of holdings meant that any payment system based on numbers of farmers would not help Britain. Politically, the absence there of a peasantry was also important. The emphasis on the CAP also resulted in a situation in which EU expenditure was not focused on programmes designed to ensure competitiveness, particularly spending on education, research and development.

This was a serious situation because the EU countries were steadily and rapidly becoming less competitive. The expansion in the world economy in the late 1980s and early 1990s, like that in the early 2000s, helped Europe, but growth did not match that in East Asia. Western Europe was affected by higher labour costs and by expensive social welfare systems, while the fiscal consequences of the reunification of West and East Germany in 1990 seriously hit the West German economy and public finances. As a clear sign of a fall in competitiveness, the percentage of trade between the member states of the EU as a percentage of their total trade rose markedly. Between 1985 and 1991, exports between its member states grew by 40 per cent, while those to other states fell by 3 per cent. This process continued in the 1990s, encouraging the currency union that led to the adoption of the Euro. Furthermore, investment in Western Europe in the 1990s rose far less than in the USA, in part because of lower productivity. Indeed, this encouraged European companies to invest in the USA and East Africa. Unemployment levels in France and Germany were far higher than in the USA, and that remains the case today. Chirac criticized Britain in 2005 on the grounds of its social system, but much of France and Germany literally was not working, and neither government had a viable solution. The same was also true of Belgium and Spain.

There were serious financial as well as economic problems in the EU. The inadequate preparations made by many Eurozone states contributed to the sharp initial devaluation of the Euro, as well as another fall in the autumn of 2000. However, in 2002, the currency was able to appreciate against the dollar. Furthermore, the responsible fiscal management decreed by the Stability and Growth Pact has not worked out. It laid down that budget deficits were not to exceed 3 per cent of the nation's annual GDP, and that national debt must be limited to 60 per cent of GDP. Failure to do so would lead to sanctions. National accounting was to be monitored from outside. These provisions did not stand the pressure of economic and budgetary problems in the early 2000s, and the political will to maintain them nationally and at the level of the EU was lacking. Portugal breached the 3 per cent deficit ceiling in 2000, followed by Germany and France in 2002, Greece in 2004, and Italy in 2005. The confusion of the EU over the issue was captured by Romano Prodi who, in November 2002, declared, 'The Stability Pact must be respected in all aspects but in such a way that economic recovery is promoted. We can consolidate the pact by interpreting and implementing its rules in an intelligent way', a remark that indicated the lack of consistency in the implementation of policy by the EU.

The tensions that arose from the Pact were demonstrated in 2004 when the French Prime Minister, Jean-Pierre Raffarin, responded to the French failure to respect the rules over deficit limits for the third year, by insisting that his 'prime duty' was to fight unemployment, not 'to produce accounting equations …so that some office or other in some country or other is satisfied'. In short, there was a tension between fighting unemployment and contributing inflation.

The Pact itself was a challenge to national sovereignty in policy-making because of the centrality of public expenditure in economic and social policy. This vindicated the arguments of British Euro-sceptics. By early 2005, the Greek deficit was about 5.3 per cent of GDP. These breaches helped ensure that opinion in states that did observe the ceiling, such as the Netherlands, Sweden and Finland, was very critical, a process accentuated by the bullying nature of German responses to the situation. Successive breaches of the deficit ceilings represented a failure of the Stability and Growth Pact that helped ensure that British adoption of the Euro would be economically *and* politically disastrous.

The failure of the Pact was made more serious by the weakness of economic growth in the Eurozone. Having risen from 2.8 per cent in 1999 to 3.5 per cent in 2000, it fell to 1.5 per cent in 2001 and 0.8 per cent in 2002. In his Budget Statement on 9 April 2003, Brown contrasted British economic performance favourably with that of the Eurozone. These problems, like the failure of the Pact, posed serious question marks against the Euro, but so also did the very nature of EMU, in particular a one-fit interest rate. This had a deflationary effect on Germany, and thus damaged economic growth in the Eurozone. The economic and financial problems were particularly acute in Italy, leading in 2005 to pressure there for devaluation and to calls for a change in EU fiscal policy or withdrawal from the Euro. By indicating that economic pressures would be blamed on the EU, this crisis helped demonstrate its weakness: it was not fundamentally grounded in consent. At the same time, the Italian solution underlined another weakness: in the absence of economic convergence, the Euro project was vulnerable to developments in individual states, particularly if they lacked fiscal discipline.

It is likely that the accession of new states to the Eurozone will cause additional problems. All ten states that joined the EU in 2004 wish to adopt the Euro. In part, these problems could be addressed by prior economic and fiscal convergence, but the ability of any system to cope with the degree of economic heterogeneity that will remain, in the context of nation-states retaining democratic politics, is unclear. So also are the results of the Euro membership for the new states, particularly the resulting lack of exchange-rate flexibility and the boom and bust situation that is likely to result. This is a serious challenge to the political stability of many states.

At the same time, the combination of politicizing and often fraudulent evasion of responsibilities and agreements seen in the deficits of the early 2000s were not new. The ERM had buckled under pressure in the early 1990s, with Italy, Spain and Portugal unable to support their currencies within the ERM, while Greece produced very questionable figures in order to qualify for Euro membership. These problems were also seen in the European core. France's ability to meet the convergence criteria rested in part on the sleight of hand involved in selling French Telecom, while the German budget for 1997 revealed a very serious fiscal crisis. Earlier, the need to cut government expenditure had led Alain Juppé, the Prime Minister appointed by Chirac in 1995, to propose cuts in expenditure that led to mass demonstrations, and helped in

1997 to lead to the defeat of his government at the election. The implications of the Stability and Growth Pact for deficit financing helped ensure rejection of the Euro in the Swedish referendum of September 2003, as the Swedes were heavily committed to their welfare system. Even the Commission President, Romano Prodi, described the Pact as 'stupid'. In practice, the provisions of the Stability and Growth Pact were both unrealizable from the outset and fudged. The row over the presidency of the European Central Bank established in 1998, which dominated the 1998 Brussels summit, was scarcely a good sign. It saw national advantage pushed to the fore, as Chirac pressed the case for Jean-Claude Trichet, Governor of the Bank of France, against the German-backed Wim Duisenberg. The latter, in 1999, became the first head of the Bank, but he had been obliged to accept a scheme designed to save Chirac's face in which he would resign the presidency before the end of his eight-year term. Duisenberg, however, refused to pledge to go on any specific date. Trichet was subsequently tried for fraud and only succeeded Duisenberg in 2003 after he had been acquitted.

Nevertheless, despite these and other problems, Blair found it difficult to publicly criticize the basis of the EU. Instead, he presented it in public as a fundamentally sound system that offered much to Britain, but required reform in order to take it forward. In a speech, 'A Clear Course for Europe', given in Cardiff on 28 November 2002, Blair declared:

> 'Today's Challenge for Europe goes to the heart of the very institutions which make up the European Union. These institutions, based on the carefully balanced triangle of Council, Commission and Parliament, underpinned by the Court of Justice, have brought Europe this far. They represent a quantum leap in democratic governance on an international scale – the pooling of sovereignty in order to extend the reach of democratic action.'

The last was not much in evidence, and Blair's remark was actively misleading.[8] His starry-eyed comments were also surprising, for example, 'It was NATO that won the Cold War, but it is the EU that will deliver the dividends of victory for generations to come.'

Optimism continued in the presentation of the constitutional change. Blair saw this as in line with British interests, and indeed declared in Warsaw in May 2003, 'If the Convention or IGC [Inter-Governmental Conference] represented a fundamental change to the British Constitution and to our system of parliamentary democracy, there would be a case for a referendum. But it doesn't.' On 20 April 2004, however, Blair told the Commons that there would indeed be a referendum, but it became clear, after the French and Dutch referenda, that he welcomed an opportunity to abandon this hostage to popularity. At the same time, his somewhat Manichean, good or evil, approach to developments left him scant room for restricting the implications and pretensions of Euro-convergence. In an interview given in May 2003, he presented the choice as 'whether we want to go forward in the European Union or not'.[9]

As so often, this was an overly simplistic account of the options. It was also one that ignored Britain's position of weakness in the EU. As enlargement progressed, so that from May 2004, there were 25, in place of 15, member countries, with more on the way, the percentage of the European Parliament held by British representatives has fallen, and the ability of Britain, or any other single country, altering outcomes determined by the EU, are nugatory.

There was also a distinct security dimension to Blair's European policy, certainly prior to the Iraq War. On 4 December 1998, at St. Malo, Britain and France pledged defence co-operation, this being seen as the key basis to a European strategic policy. The Euro-fighter, however, revealed that such co-operation was as redundant in practical military terms as the Iraq War suggested it was in policy matters. Already, in the Bosnia and Kosovo crises of the 1990s, Britain and France had found themselves bearing most of the European military burden. Furthermore, the reduction in military expenditure by other EU states, such as Germany, suggested that even if there was a united response in future crises, Britain would bear a disproportionate share. The widespread unwillingness to spend on defence reflects a misleading EU confidence that it will be possible to be more influential than the USA, precisely because the EU is more reliant on diplomacy than force. Ironically, this is an approach that depends on an underpinning of American strength.[10]

The divisions caused by the Iraq War made a mockery of the idea of co-operating over issues such as the projected European Rapid Reaction Force, although it did not prevent the continued flood of new initiatives. Thus, in a summit in September 2003, Blair signed up to the proposals of Chirac and Schröder for a united military force able to act independently of NATO. This followed a meeting held at Tervuren in Belgium, in April 2003, in which France, Germany, Belgium and Luxembourg agreed to establish a European military union. The EU Armaments Agency established in 2004 set up initiatives including the creation of advanced communication systems and the development of unmanned drones; initiatives that duplicated American policies and challenged NATO co-operation. Galileo, the European-proposed alternative to the American GPS system, was particularly controversial as China was included as a partner. This was seen in the USA as at one with the proposal to end the European arms embargo imposed on China after the suppression of the pro-democracy movement in 1989. Unlike the USA, the EU has no real role in the management of East Asian developments. From the American perspective, European arms sales can therefore be seen as a dangerous form of meddling. The EU's capacity to help manage international developments was badly dented in August 2005, when Iran reopened its plant at Isfahan in order to resume uranium conversion, a procedure that might eventually result in the production of a nuclear weapon. European negotiations had been designed to define a sphere between American policy and Islamic intransigence, but it lacked any real force to give substance to the negotiations in the event of the rejection of this mediation.

An EU in conflict with America's interests is not one in

accord with Britain's, but that is the direction driven by France and the capability sought by Brussels. The Euro was explicitly intended as a rival to the dollar, with international political benefits supposed to flow from this position. Although some American policies are inappropriate for Britain and the EU, the backing for Turkish entry being particularly so, there is an essential alignment of common concern.

Given Blair's willingness to sponsor large-scale constitutional changes within Britain, it is scarcely surprising that he has been ready to accept others as far as relations within the EU are concerned. This has been downplayed because of an emphasis on remaining outside the Euro, but this neglects the insidious and cumulative process of change during the Blair governments, and the extent to which this is disguised is particularly troubling. In part, this is a matter of the incorporation of European assumptions or requirements in British legislation or government practice. The trace is not always clear, but, nevertheless, exists. For example, the support for regional government owes much to a commitment to this level by the EU. Ironically, when put to the public in a referendum in the North-East of England, this policy was soundly rejected. This was symptomatic of a more widespread public reluctance about constitutional innovation, seen, for example, in the very narrow majority in favour of the establishment of a Welsh Assembly in the referendum held in 1997.

The Blair governments made little attempt to defend national interests understood in terms of the competence of British electors and jurors to affect their future through Parliament and the legal system. This was seen before the 2005 election when it was made known from Brussels that if the Conservatives were elected they would not be able to implement their proposals on asylum and immigration, as they clashed with treaty agreements entered into by Labour. Whatever the views of the latter on the particular provisions, they ought to have taken a robust attitude in defence of the ability of electors, via the parliamentary system, to define national interests. This is a direct way to engage with the public and to address the democratic deficit, but this was not Labour's way.

Blair does not only seem to find it difficult to define and defend British interests. He also appears to find the same problem with Europe in that he has not given a coherent account of its identity. This is readily apparent with Blair's eager support for Turkish accession to the EU: the Commission, indeed, decided in December 2004 to recommend opening accession talks with Turkey. This would take Europe to the borders of Georgia, Armenia, Iran, Iraq and Syria, and bring in a society whose average income is considerably lower than the rest of Europe. In 2002, Edmund Stoiber, the Prime Minister of Bavaria, who narrowly lost the election for the German Chancellorship, argued that Turkish accession would be an excessive fiscal, and therefore economic, burden. Turkey's culture is also different in many respects, as shown by the criminalization of adultery there. Furthermore, in 2005 the European Commission warned Turkey that a draft law on religious institutions did not meet EU standards on religious freedom. The population of Turkey – about 71 million – and its high growth rate when contrasted with the lower growth rate of Germany, whose population is now about 82 million, is such that, if admitted, it would become the most populous EU state by about 2020, with only the possibility of Russian entry able to dispel this. Demographic strength would be accompanied by voting rights. Although the EU has ruled out accession for the North African members of Euromed, Muslim demographic weight will be further accentuated if Albania and Bosnia join the EU. This would lead, depending on Turkish growth rates, to Muslim-majority states having about 122 million people out of an EU population of about 587 million, and the latter will also include the approximately 15 million Muslims in the 25 states of the 2005 EU. Moldova and Ukraine have both expressed a wish to join the EU, which will lessen the Muslim percentage, although only modestly.

Arguments can be made for and against Turkish entry, but Blair has not offered a coherent explanation of Europe in terms of Turkish membership. Angela Merkel, the German CDU leader and recently-elected Chancellor, has provided a far more cogent analysis, one in which there is an argument for the close relations of a 'privileged partnership', but not accession. The value of anchoring the lands to the east of the bulk of the EU in terms of democracy and stability is clear, but it is far less clear that countries such as Albania, Belarus, Bosnia, Russia, Turkey and Ukraine would pose anything less than very serious, and possibly insuperable, problems for the EU.

Dissension over Turkish entry interacted with other tensions within the EU. In August 2005, Dominique de Villepin, the recently-appointed French Prime Minister, declared that it was 'inconceivable' that Turkey could begin accession talks without recognizing Cyprus. When, as a condition of accession talks, the Turkish government signed the protocol extending its customs union with the EU to the new members that had joined in 2004 including Cyprus, it issued a statement that this did not imply recognition of the Greek-Cypriot government. In 1974, a Turkish invasion followed an unsuccessful coup by Greek Cypriots keen on union with Greece, and, after 'ethnic cleansing', led to the creation of a *de facto* independent Turkish-Cypriot statelet in the north of the island. This has since been sustained, and there has been no unification to match that of Germany, understandably so as the divisions in Cyprus run more deeply. In April 2004, in a referendum, the Greek Cypriots voted heavily against a UN reunification plan that had been seen by the EU as important to accession. The Turkish Cypriots, in contrast, voted in favour. In 2004, however, the EU accepted the accession of Cyprus in terms of the Greek-Cypriot government part of the island. The EU saw this as the sole legitimate representative of the island and, in light of the wish to speed Cypriot accession, allowed it to accede accordingly without having first reached a settlement with the Turkish-Cypriot statelet.

This was not intended as a bar to Turkish accession, and Turkish recognition of Cyprus was not selected as a precondition for Turkish accession talks. Instead, in a clear response to the weakness of the EU, a weakness accentuated by the extent to which the USA is best placed to influence Turkish policy, the status of the island was 'parked' by being left to discussions under the auspices of the United Nations. However, prior to the accession talks, which Blair is very keen to forward, not least because of his concerns over the Middle East, all the EU states have to agree a framework for discussions. The Turkish government refused to respond to French pressure, and declared that it was unwilling to accept the precondition of recognizing Cyprus. This position was supported by the European enlargement Commissioner, Olli Rehn, who, in August 2005, declared that new conditions could not be set for entry talks. While accurate in terms of the diplomatic background, this was not an approach that bore much relationship to public views. Austrian consent was obtained only with considerable difficulty in October 2005.

The issue is of importance not simply because of the serious consequences likely to result from Turkish membership, but also as it indicates the degree to which there is not only a lack of political unity between Britain and France, but, in fact, active rivalry. In part, the new-found strength and bitterness of this rivalry stems from the Iraq crisis of 2002-3, and the fact that the leaders of both Britain and France during that crisis are still in power. Turkish accession to the EU is appropriately linked to this, because Blair and the American government see it as a way to encourage Turkey to remain pro-Western. Thus, a key aspect of European policy has been annexed to a highly contentious Middle Eastern policy. Indeed, American pressure on the EU in 2002-3 to speed Turkish accession was directly linked to hopes of winning Turkish support in the Iraq War. Blair is also anxious to show that a progressive Islamic state is not a contradiction in terms. Furthermore, as more generally with Blair, for example over his enthusiasm for joining the Euro, there is a concern with aspirations rather than practicalities. The problems likely to stem from Turkish accession negotiations, let alone Turkish accession, have been largely brushed aside in order to focus on the apparently higher goal.

The Labour manifesto for the 2005 election claimed that the constitution 'sets out what the EU can do and what it cannot', and therefore is 'a good treaty for Britain and for the new Europe'. This was a noteworthy comment on the votes by British MEPs on 12 January 2005, when the Parliament voted by 500 to 137 in favour of a positive report on the constitution, but the British MEPs who voted did so by 40 to 29 against. The Labour manifesto was also ironic in light of how the government subsequently responded after the French negative.

Blair sees himself as the solution to problems, whether with his support for Turkish membership helping to ease Middle East and Muslim tensions, or, more generally, able to offer the leadership the EU needs to address its problems. Instead, he is part of the problem, yet fails to appreciate this. This is the case both with specifics and in more general terms. As far as the first is concerned, the legacy of the Iraq War has limited domestic confidence in Blair's assurances, and has left his relations with many European politicians in tatters. This is accentuated by continuing anxieties over the policy of President Bush, to whom he is seen as overly close. There are also his longstanding poor relations with Chirac, each, with reason, finding the other hypocritically sententious and overly facile.

In general terms, Blair, however, is more of a problem because, as the contention over joining the Euro made clear, he puts a consistent emphasis on vision and politics over practicalities and government. This is most acute in terms of his general ignorance of economics and his failure to put sufficient weight on economic factors. As such, Blair is in a long line of politicians who sponsored and supported the European project, including, most obviously, in Britain Heath, and elsewhere, Mitterrand, Kohl and Delors, and more recently, Prodi. None understood that their preference for political symbolism and structures would not win public acceptance, let alone support, if they could not create the appropriate economic fundamentals. Major's support for Maastricht can be seen in the same perspective, but he was less naïve than Heath. He did not so much neglect economic factors as fail to manage them. A lack of public acceptance was demonstrated in the EU elections in 2004, in which less than half the electorate voted, and that despite the compulsory nature of the vote in four of the member states.

A failure to move slowly and to build from the economic

fundamentals was abundantly seen with the Euro and with the mishandling of the economics of German re-unification. The latter is an appropriate parallel, as, in many respects, the EU rested similarly on a post-World War Two idealism, and German re-unification was a key aspect of the end of the war. Yet, the political sense of rebirth and the specific pressure to create a new solution was not appropriate in the 1980s and 1990s for already-functioning societies and economies, and the same is true today, however much Blair tries to offer visionary leadership. To get the EU to work, if it can, requires the patient pursuit of changes in labour and social welfare assumptions and regulations. This is best handled at the national level, because it is there that political leadership is most potent and expected, and there, especially in France and Germany, that the assumptions focus. This is not a course that Blair with his careless enthusiasms will accept. Instead, he falls within the pattern of feckless leadership that has helped to discredit the EU. Seeking steadily greater powers is not the best response to problems, and will help make the EU even more unable to fulfil its own goals and more sclerotic, both of which will create a sense of dissatisfaction.

If Blair is an aspect of the problem, he is also on the way out. Despite winning re-election and being in a stronger domestic position than Berlusconi, Chirac or Merkel, Blair's announcement that he would not stand again for election has helped make him appear a fading asset, if not yet a lame duck. This will be accentuated with signs of ministers manoeuvring to replace him in Britain. A gesture-politician whose gestures are running out, Blair did not translate into an effective director of government able to ensure long-term improvements, and this is equally true of the European as of the British scale.

1 B. Vogler and J. Voss (eds.), *Strasbourg, Schoepflin et l'Europe au XVIIIe siècle* (Bonn, 1996).
2 G. Savage, 'Favier's heirs: the French Revolution and the *Secret du Roi*', *Historical Journal*, 41 (1998), pp. 225-58; T. E. Kaiser, 'Who's Afraid of Marie-Antoinette? Diplomacy, Austrophobia and the Queen', *French History*, 14 (2000), pp. 241-71.

3 K. M. Baker, 'Politique et opinion publique sous l'ancien régime', *Annales*, 42 (1987), pp. 41-71.
4 Presentation on 'Culture and Identity' to Agora think-tank, London, 21 October 2004; Gove, 'Killing the state on the battlefield of ideas', *The Times*, 7 November 2000.
5 R. Broad, *Labour's European Dilemmas From Bevin to Blair* (Basingstoke, 2001).
6 R. Peston, *Brown's Britain* (London, 2005).
7 *Sunday Telegraph*, 16 January 2005, article by Robert Peston.
8 P. Morgan, *Alarming Drum. Britain's European Dilemma* (Exeter, 2005), p. 39.
9 *Financial Times*, 29 May 2003.
10 R. Kagan, *Paradise and Power: America and Europe in the New World Order* (New York, 2003).

CHAPTER 6

FUTURE SCENARIOS

Discussion of the future is apt to be dominated by the immediate aftermath of the present. Writing in November 2005, this means a focus on the likely consequences of the French and Dutch refusals, in popular referenda, to ratify the new European constitution, and the likely results of this, both for the constitution, which now appears dead, certainly in its present form; and also for Europe more generally. The constitution was drafted by the Convention for the Future of Europe under the chairmanship of Valéry Giscard d'Estaing, who had his own ambitions to be a President of Europe. The constitution was accepted in June 2004 by the European summit in Dublin. It represented a major shift towards re-creating the EU as a quasi-state. Article I-5 required member states 'to facilitate the achievement of the Union's tasks and refrain from any measure which could jeopardise the attainment of the Union's objective'. Furthermore, the implications in particular areas were striking. For example, in the field of foreign policy, the individual member states were expected to comply with Union policy: 'before undertaking any action on the international scene or any commitment which could affect the Union's interests, each Member State shall consult the others within the European Council' (article I-40(5)). The European Court of Justice (ECJ) would gain jurisdiction over foreign and security policy. In short, a major area of sovereignty would be lost. Furthermore, the codification of the primacy of EU law would have ensured that the ECJ, which was to be renamed The Court of Justice, in practice became a European supreme court.

Detailed provisions were far more intrusive, and in effect left national governments with limited functions; a rejection, in practice, of the theory of subsidiarity outlined in the Maastricht Treaty, as well as of the goal for the constitution outlined at the EU summit at Laeken in December 2001, bringing the EU closer to 'its' citizens. It was this summit that established the Convention for the Future of Europe. The Commission's duty under the constitution to 'co-ordinate economic policies' in effect created a right to end what would be seen as national variations. 'Public health' was also established as an EU competence under the constitution, which provided for 'supporting, co-ordinating or complementary' action in health, education, vocational training, culture, youth and sport, a process of extension that provided opportunities for recasting much of the fabric of sociability. Provisions for the EU's 'area of freedom, security and justice', and for a European Public Prosecutor (a provision in which the objection by the British government was overruled), as well as the European Arrest Warrant which came into force on 1 January 2004, were intimations of a federal police and justice system. The constitution decreed 'approximation of the laws and the regulations of the Member States' in criminal matters having 'a cross-border dimension'. The prospect of judicial harmonization was particularly threatening to the few states with common law traditions: Britain, Ireland and Malta. For Britain, these traditions are more generally crucial to the character of national political culture and to national identity.

By making the provisions of the European Charter of Fundamental Rights compulsory, the constitution's guarantees, for example of the right to strike, to paid leave and to limited working hours, while apparently reasonable, also strengthened the regulatory nature of the provisions.[1] This was taken forward by an emphasis on the welfare state rather than the state as the facilitator of individual freedom and liberties. Indeed, the objectives outlined in the constitution directly threatened such liberties, not only because they entailed more regulation, an aspect of large-scale redistribution of resources, but also further such redistribution through taxation. Indeed, the constitution reflected a fundamental failure to understand the values of individualism.

Furthermore, the vagueness of much of the language, for example the right to 'dignity', provided much scope for judicial activism, interpretative creep and spreading regulation. Such a description may seem emotive but is, in practice, an accurate description of the process by which the scope of European institutions has expanded.

The constitution, ludicrously, but all too typically, misleadingly, described by the Blair government as simply a 'tidying up exercise', was intended as the departure point for a new process of institutional expansion. For example, a Fundamental Rights Agency was to ascertain if rights endorsed in the constitution were being defended. This offered the possibility of reviewing practice in all spheres of life. In light of such proposals, it is scarcely surprising that Miguel Anel Moratinos, Spain's Foreign Minister, remarked of the constitution, 'We are witnessing the last remnants of national politics.' The proposals for majority voting are a major compromise of the national dimension, for example over criminal justice and immigration. This was presented as a guarantee of necessary efficiency.

The results of each referendum were far more striking than had been anticipated. It had been very possible that each would lead to a rejection, but it was also possible that the impact would have been lessened as a result either of a low turnout or of a very close result, or indeed, of both. Neither was the case. Turnout was high: 70 per cent in France on 29 May and 63 per cent in the Netherlands on 1 June, percentages that compared favourably with other European elections and indeed with the 42.3 per cent turnout in the Spanish referendum on 20 January. Furthermore, this was the first Dutch referendum.

The results were far from close, as had also been the case in Spain, where 77 per cent voted for the constitution. The majority in France against was close to 10 per cent of the votes cast, and in the Netherlands still higher: 55 per cent of the French voters and 61.6 per cent of the Dutch voted no. In the USA, this would be regarded as a landslide, while British governments rely on percentages of votes cast far smaller than either figure. Although in Luxembourg on 10 July there was subsequently a referendum result in favour of the constitution, the percentage that voted against (43) was surprisingly high, given the country's long support for the EU: it gains more per capita from the EU than any other member state. One of the most amusing moments of recent politics was provided by Jean-Claude Juncker, the Prime Minister, declaring that the result was 'every bit as important as those in France and the Netherlands'. The results in France and the Netherlands were particularly impressive because there was no major Euro-sceptic political party in either country, and the campaigns were largely mounted from scratch.

As with all elections, the battles for the vote were followed by the struggle to 'spin' the results. To blame failure on what is despised and/or regarded as anachronistic is one of the regrettable skills of news-management, and this was seen in full after the referenda. It was most apparent in France, but was also the case in Brussels and among Euro-enthusiasts elsewhere, not least in Britain. President Chirac had chosen the course of a referendum, which was not necessary in legal terms, in order to strengthen the government, marginalize critics within the right-wing, and harm the divided Socialists, who were publicly divided on the merits of the constitution. The Deputy Leader, Laurent Fabius, a former Prime Minister, campaigned against the constitution, in defiance of the Party line, and this accentuated the division. Chirac's policy was part of a familiar process in which the European issue was used by governments in an attempt to divide and discredit oppositions, not least by applying charges of populism and extremism. Having badly misread the likely trajectory of electoral opinion, and ironically so because of his failure also to do so with the National Assembly results in 1997, Chirac then blamed the result on popular anger with economic conditions. In failing to address the question of why this anger should focus on the EU constitution, the arrogant Chirac characteristically infantilized the electorate, assuming that they were only capable of blind spasms of anger. His attitude contrasted with that of de Gaulle, the last French leader to lose a referendum: he resigned, with considerable dignity, in 1969.

As so often, Chirac demonstrates that those who support the European 'project', by their assumptions denigrate the exercise of the popular will. This was also seen in the argument that the voters did not understand the projected constitution, and therefore voted in ignorance, an approach that made it almost necessary to ignore and/or seek to reverse their verdict. Again, this approach is problematic in particulars and all too indicative of attitudes in general terms. It is also an attitude that is not adopted when there is backing for the popular mandate. If the French and Dutch are supposed to have voted out of ignorance or selfish interests, it is not clear what to make of the Spaniards who voted yes to the constitution in a referendum on 20 February 2005. The French referendum was seen as key and, far from there being widespread ignorance, large numbers of copies of the constitution had been provided free by its supporters. Furthermore, there was extensive debate, in print and in public meetings, about France and the EU. The propaganda effort was considerable, and stemmed from within France and from Brussels. In the former case, the government used the agencies of the state to support the yes vote, which was also backed by the leading opposition party, the Socialists, the leading employer and trade union organizations, the Catholic Church, and most of the television channels, newspapers and magazines. The European Commission and Parliament also spent substantial sums on what can only be described as propaganda, which, of course, was funded from taxes. Public opinion polls indicated, however, that as knowledge of the constitution increased and the debate became more insistent, so opposition hardened and became more popular.

Clearly, alongside anxiety about the constitution, or aspects of it, hostility to the governments of Chirac and Jan Peter Balkenende also played a role in the referenda. Indeed, the lesson for politicians was that verdicts on their performance will necessarily characterize EU referenda, as the nature of the process is that whatever are referred to referenda will be EU agreements in which national governments have participated. The risk of rejection will encourage the avoidance or manipulation of referenda. This will be an aspect of the democratic deficit so potent within the EU.

Hostility to change and challenge also played a major role in the rejection, and this will further encourage the democratic deficit just mentioned. The EU constitution was seen as symbolizing the extent to which, behind the fig-leaf of pooling sovereignty, individual countries had lost control of their destinies, and thus a hostile view of how the EU operated and was tending became a prism through which past, present and future could be assessed. Alongside a loss of power by individual countries, the EU represented a transfer of power to government (both ministers and bureaucrats) and away from the scrutiny of legislatures, and thus the popular political process. The Danes have proved particularly alert to this shift. It is most pronounced when ministers attend summits, reach agreements, and present them to domestic legislatures as *faits accomplis*. Indeed, the process of revision is far from easy, and this is even more the case now that agreements have been reached by twenty-five states.

In specific terms, the issues raised in the referenda in 2005 included the movement of jobs and labour which have been encouraged by the freedoms offered by the EU, particularly as a consequence of enlargement, but which, anyway, would have played a major role as an aspect of the varied processes referred to as globalization. The vocabulary employed in France and elsewhere revealed a particular unwillingness to accept the notion of change. Referring to the competition of labour in other states, that is cheaper as a consequence of less social welfare or of lower wages, as 'social dumping' prejudges the issues, as does the description of protectionism as a 'unique market model'. Thatcher correctly focused on issues of vocabulary, and the potent nature of the conceptionalization of interests in such phrases indicates why Blair is unlikely to win his struggle for reform. This is not least because, with his own fascination with spin, he is overly willing to allow words and phrases to mean what they seem, rather than to apply a rigorous analysis of them. An ultimate post-modernist in politics, Blair is not therefore suited to confront the obfuscations of the EU.

At the same time, as in domestic policy, there is a major

problem with implementation, specifically a striking contrast between Blair's support for EU reform and the reality of what he has delivered. This can be seen with his support for science and research as a modernizing cause of prosperity and a replacement for the CAP. Indeed, in 2000, at the Lisbon summit, Blair agreed to join in a doubling to 3 per cent of European research spending as a proportion of GDP. In practice, Britain has pitifully failed to increase its share, which was 1.8 per cent in 2003, less than the EU average let alone the higher percentages in France, Germany and the USA. The British government has failed to provide leadership or appropriate incentives for the private sector.

France's investment in applied research is more impressive than that of Britain, and provides a different viewpoint from the usual emphasis on reactionary French attitudes and policies. Nevertheless, the role of cheap labour within Europe is a particular challenge to French conceptions of the EU, which, from 1957, already focused on the debilitating social welfare provisions of a Social Chapter.[2] Competition from cheap labour brings home the consequences both of new member states and of the nature of the modern economy at every level. The importance of French rejection in the referendum was an aspect of the marginalization of Britain. Had Britain voted no then it would have been argued that it was only to be expected, that one state could not thwart the others, and that Britain must not vote again. Jean-Claude Juncker, the Luxembourg Prime Minister, and the then EU President, indeed said in Paris on 19 April that the constitution would not be blocked if France voted against it: 'There will be no renegotiating of the treaty if a country says no… We will pursue the ratification process, although it is true that ratifications following a "no" from one member state would become increasingly difficult.' Juncker also argued that rejection would make the USA more powerful, an indication of the widespread view among supporters of the EU, particularly in France, Belgium and Luxembourg, that it should counter the USA. Blair believed that he could bridge the gap between the EU and the USA by having Britain join the Euro as a way to satisfy EU doubts about the Anglo-American alignment, and to demonstrate that he was able to offer a vision of Britain's place in Europe different to that alleged by Chirac and Schröder. This belief, however, rested on a serious fallacy about the views of much of the EU 'political class'. It also reflected Blair's instrumentalist approach to the British electorate, and his preference for tactical finesse over substantive statesmanship based on a profound understanding of national interests.

In 2005, the Iran issue posed a further challenge to Blair's attempt to bridge the EU and the USA. Schröder deliberately used the issue in his attempt to win the election. Opposition to the USA is a major difference between Britain and *some* of the EU, and one that is far deeper than differences over policy in the Middle East, although they were important. Michel Barnier, French Foreign Minister in 2004-5, declared 'our American friends must understand that we are going to build Europe, not only as a market but as a power'. The British do not fight to protect their language from Americanisms as the French do. Legislation of 1975 and 1994 banning the use of foreign words in official documents, advertising and packaging if there are French alternatives is indicative of a troubling mixture of hubris, stubbornness and lack of confidence. Another instructive contrast is provided by cultural aspects of trade liberalization, with the French devoting much energy to subsidizing their cinema and to resisting American cuisine.

Juncker was not alone. At the European Summit on 16 June 2005, Schröder, in line with what he had agreed with Chirac in Berlin on 4 June, stated that the meeting could 'give advice, but it cannot break off the ratification processes or rule in what form, in what time frames they should take place'. Balkenende took the same line. However, the summit agreed to shelve the timetable for ratification, to review it in 2006 and to allow member states to decide whether to hold referenda: Luxembourg decided to do so, but Britain, the Czech Republic, Denmark, Ireland, Poland and Portugal announced indefinite postponements of referenda and Finland and Sweden of parliamentary votes. The notion of allowing states to decide whether to hold referenda was all too indicative of the undemocratic and top-down nature of the EU. The British government had already announced on 6 June that the referendum plans had been shelved; although Jack Straw kept the option open for 2006. This is troubling in terms of the repeated integrationist tendency of British policy under Labour, one that is somewhat concealed by the failure to join the Euro.

While instructive, the process of focusing on the future needs to be complemented by a consideration of the long-term, and it is at this level of analysis that uncertainty particularly prevails, both over challenges, their character, intensity, interaction and timing, and over likely responses and their impact. Most of the key problems of the future will not be restricted to Europe, and the extent to which European institutions will be able to mount a viable response in furtherance, or in the absence, of a wider solution, is far from clear. It is increasingly likely that the pace and extent of human impact on the environment is such that the most serious challenges to the future of the species will be environmental in character, specifically arising from the degradation of the environment and from issues of resource availability, particularly energy and water. Both became prominent in 2005 as oil prices rose, while much of Europe, not least large parts of France and Spain, faced drought without any sign of policies to improve the future situation. There is no sign that the EU has anything particular to offer in environment policy.

A related, but far from co-terminous, challenge is posed by the prospect of serious diseases killing large numbers. Although international co-operation is necessary to deal with this threat, it is far from clear that EU institutions represent the best form for this co-operation. Instead, action at the European level will probably operate in place of the potentially more effective nature of the individual state, although proponents of change who despair of support at the national level, for example for nuclear power, may seek a European solution in order to take advantage of the space created by the democratic deficit.

Compared to these challenges, those from political threats are less serious. Of the latter, the most obviously present at the moment arises from militant Islam, not least because of the presence of large and fast-growing numbers of Muslims in Europe and their increased activism and refusal to accept democratic results. This issue can be differently posed by suggesting that it represents, in the most telling form, the extent to which the identities represented by religious commitment have not abated and, instead, that the account of progress understood as secularism (and state control) requires revision. From this perspective, Christian activism may, indeed, present a threat alongside radical Islam. That may seem far-fetched, but the history of Northern Ireland in recent decades serves as a reminder that bloody sectarianism can also be based in competing senses of Christian identity.

Nevertheless, it would be foolish to detract attention from the far more serious threat posed by radical Islam. Indeed, that played a role in the referenda in France and the Netherlands in 2005 and would also have played a role had one been permitted in Britain. Voters registered their concern about the prospect of Turkish entry, while the Dutch were also anxious because the Common European Asylum Policy has made it difficult to strengthen their asylum regulations in response to large-scale public anxiety about Islamic activism. The Conservatives correctly drew attention to the same issue in 2005 but failed to make sufficient electoral headway from it.

If future challenges for the EU can be differently defined, the nature and calibre of likely responses are, unsurprisingly, unclear. As far as Britain is concerned, analysts who detect, indeed sometimes welcome, signs of weakness, are most prone to argue the need for a different political framework. This thesis is most relevant to those who feel frustrated and thwarted by the British state, most obviously nationalist movements in Scotland, Wales and Northern Ireland. This process was accentuated by crises within British institutions in the 1990s and by the pressure for change that led to the efflorescence of New Labour. Although the movement's ambition to address national and international problems knew few constraints (and rejected experience), its ability to do so proved far more limited. The superficial character of New Labour and its failure to achieve its stated goals on the European scale were apparent before the multiple political blows of 2002-5: first the Iraq War and then differences over the best way to 'reform' Europe made it clear that British-led leadership would be greatly contested.

At the same time, the alternatives are weak. The EU takes sufficient authority and power from the constituent states to make it impossible for them both to solve problems on their own, and also difficult for them to co-operate unless through the auspices of the EU institutions; but these very institutions lack the credibility, ability and support to provide solutions, and have repeatedly been found wanting. Thus, the radical problems posed by environmental and other challenges cannot best be addressed by the checks and balances of the EU, and it is very unlikely that the situation will be improved if the EU institutions are less constrained. At the same time, the practice of responsible government at the national level is being eroded, not least because of the loss of fiscal control to the European Central Bank; while the rampant fraud that has led the European Court of Auditors repeatedly to refuse to approve the EU accounts (in November 2004 for the tenth successive year) also suggests that the EU – both its processes and its absence of self-regulation – is inherently not only corrupt but also corrupting. The extent to which this refusal is not a highly-contentious public scandal is surprising, but also reflects the lack of idealism focused on the EU. Much of the fraud focuses on the CAP, which is not only a policy mistake, but also a source of more widespread corruption. Fraud, however, is also more wide-ranging. In 1999, the Cresson affair led to the fall of the Santer Commission, and in 2003 fraud within Eurostat, the Commission's statistical body, hit the Prodi Commission.

Financial fraud, however, paled into insignificance beside its political counterpart or, possibly, should be seen as symptomatic of the latter. This political fraud was seen not only in misleading analyses and predictions, designed to ensure that the integrationist 'project' remained unimpeachable, but also in the suppression of reports that might lead to the qualification of EU initiatives. This was persistently seen during successive enlargement processes. Misleading accounts of the accession states were not challenged and critical EU reports were kept secret. For example, in 2003, the European Parliament was not informed about a negative EU report on the politically partisan nature of the Polish judiciary as it was feared that this might affect the enlargement vote.

Posing long-term issues provides a context for looking at the current conception of the future, which is largely defined by the issue of how best to respond to the rejection of the European constitutional treaty by the French and Dutch electorates. After an election, commentators rush to explain results, and generally over-simplify the situation, but there does seem to be a contrast between French criticism of the process of European change as threatening to dissolve social safety, and Dutch views about the overweening demands of the EU.

If, however, hostility to the real, or apparent, pretensions and activities of the EU comes from different sources, and much was made by Euro-enthusiasts about contrasts between French and Dutch views, this does not imply that the EU is an appropriate *via media* or necessary compromise, both views voiced by supporters of Euro-convergence. Such an approach accords with a tendency to see different views to those of Euro-convergence in terms of factious opposition that necessarily needs to be ignored or overridden, a view that is in accord both with the 'official mind' of the EU and also with a centrist, or generally left-of-centre, political alignment. Politically, this attitude is at variance with the Anglo-American practice and precept of shifts in government control with the concomitant understanding not only that opposition is constitutionally valid, but also that its political place includes the role of gaining power.

The standard approach of the official EU mind also neglects the extent to which differences in opinion at the level of individual countries does not prove any need to concentrate authority at the EU level, in order to prevent chaos understood as an absence of consistency. Instead, it is appropriate, in a democratic context, both for decisions to be reached at the level of these countries, and for the system to be sufficiently flexible to allow for these differences leading to significant divergences in policy. If the French wish to take a different line on economic liberalism, that ought to be a matter for their people and government, and therefore for their own tax payers and legislators.

Such an approach is anathema, not just to those who are defined as seeking a super-state, but also to supporters of the single market who took its logic to be that of a focus on decision-making at the EU level. The economic logic might well point to that, but the democratic habit does not. Indeed, many of the forthcoming scenarios are affected by likely clashes between economic pressures and democratic views. The two are far from separate, as the force of consumerism and the fear of unemployment indicates, but there is a major tension that is linked to time-scales, perceptions, and levels of decision-making.

In many respects, the EU is a system created in order to nullify democratic pressures, specifically populist ones. In part, this was a response to history, specifically to the role of political extremism in overturning order, stability and freedom across much of Europe (but not Britain) earlier in the twentieth century, and, in part, a product of concern about the strength of right-wing extremism in recent decades. As such, the EU is a system that should have been conducive to introducing potentially unpopular economic policies, such as the single market. This was certainly the case in the 1980s, but in the 2000s, it has proved less the case. This reflects both the growing strength of democratic demands and the failure, both in absolute and relative terms, of the EU to deliver the economic growth, prosperity and sense of security its citizens anticipated, and, increasingly, vociferously demanded, not least because social mobility seems no longer to be largely an upward process.

The strength of democratic demands will not dissipate, not least because populism received a powerful accretion from the overthrow of authoritarian Communist regimes in Eastern

Europe, a process that continued with the peaceful transition in Ukraine in 2005. The end of the Cold War and the subsequent expansion of the EU has proved a challenge, not only because of the difficulties of assimilating very different economies, but also because the anti-authoritarian populism seen in Eastern Europe, which played such a powerful role in the overthrow of Communism, remains a potent factor, and has normative value due to its role in the fall of the Iron Curtain.

Throughout Europe, populism poses an acute political problem for the EU, one shown clearly in the case of referenda. The German government, for example, decided not to have a referendum on the constitution. If decision-making is handled at the EU level, then, whether or not it is complemented by a major role for the European Parliament, there is the danger that populism interacts with nationalism, the two fusing to pose a serious challenge to legitimacy and, consequently, to stability. The alternative is to leave considerable power to national governments and parliaments, which are the bodies best placed to respond to, engage with, and if necessary, contain populist pressures. Such an attempt to address the democratic deficit will make the negotiation of compromises at the level of the EU more difficult, but may be the sole way to address the problem.

This, however, creates problems for Britain. On 1 July 2005, when Britain began its six months in the EU's rotating presidency, José Manuel Barroso, the Commission's President, responded to Blair's call to re-examine the EU's social model in order to update it to encourage growth, by expressing support, but also adding as a general point, 'No one is going to impose its own point of view on the others.' He also pressed for a 'culture of compromise' and the avoidance of 'nationalist rhetoric' which he claimed would 'get Europe nowhere', but this ignored the extent to which the current basis of such a culture hindered any attempt at reform in a British conception, or possibly in any other.

From a functional viewpoint, any process of compromise may seem to make it more difficult for Europe to compete at the international level and to respond to challenges. The geopolitical approach of the EU, as part of a system of competing blocs, leads to this view. Both, however, suffer from the fallacy that a top-down approach is the best, and from the assumption that government necessarily proposes and presents the solution. This is very much in accordance with the statist nature of Continental political culture and the interventionist practice of corporatist governmental systems, but it is unclear that they work well, and it is certainly the case that they differ from the assumptions that underlay the major shifts in British government in the 1980s.

It is in this context that the position of Blair and his government during the negotiations for the constitution, needs to be considered. Support for the European constitution had been pushed hard by Blair in early 2005. In February, the Second Reading of the European Union Bill passed the Commons by 345 to 140, and the Conservative amendment was rejected by 348 to 131. Commitment to the constitution was clearly expressed in the Labour general election manifesto, and both this and the parliamentary debate are worth re-reading in light of the subsequent referenda results. Blair was clearly hoping that a referendum would be successful, not least in the aftermath of the constitution's passage elsewhere.

Then, the successive rejections of the projected European constitution by the French and Dutch electorates led to a burst of euphoria among British Euro-sceptics and appeared to create a bond of interest between them and those who supported a less intrusive European Union. Blair adeptly managed this. By declaring that the constitution would not be put to the British electorate, he removed himself from the position of being a serious hostage to fortune that the promise of such a referendum had threatened. Furthermore, he enjoyed a considerable upsurge in bipartisan popularity, with support, albeit not uncritical support, expressed by politicians of very different views, such as Michael Howard in the Commons, and the spokesman for the UK Independence Party in the European Parliament.

However attractive Blair's position might be to Eurosceptics, if the choice is between his position and that of

Chirac and the former German Chancellor Schröder, the situation, however, is far less comfortable. This is for two reasons: firstly, what Blair himself has said, and secondly, a consideration of his likely tactics when faced by obduracy on the part of European partners and by problems elsewhere in the world. As far as Blair's remarks are concerned, it is readily apparent that his hostility to Chirac and Schröder, partly a product of personal anger over Iraq as much as over Europe, represents opposition to a particular conception of the EU, but opposition expressed from a conviction that the EU is a vital interest for Britain, and that being in the EU is a key definition of New Labour. The last is an important point, for much of Blair's policy still rests on an instructive reaction against the policies and views of Old Labour, some of which, ironically, he supported in his early days in politics. Support for the EU serves Blair as another instance of his classic commitment to a *via media* in politics. It enables New Labour to be distanced from the Old Labour Euro-scepticism of a Tony Benn, as well as from the Euro-scepticism associated with the Tories. Furthermore, these distinctions serve to validate the project in his eyes.

On 23 June 2005, when Blair addressed the European Parliament, he announced: 'I am a passionate pro-European', as well as referring positively to the concept of Europe as a 'political project' and 'a union of values'. It was not the occasion to mention that, in assumption and practice, these were frequently not the same as British values, but the reference to a political project is certainly a departure from the commitment to a looser Europe that has so often been emphasized by British politicians.

Furthermore, in terms of tactics, there is a willingness on the part of Blair to offer concessions that again suggested a desire to please. He stated in June 2005 that he was the sole British leader ever to declare that he was willing to negotiate over the British rebate, an issue that Michael Howard had earlier raised. Furthermore, although critical of the CAP, which involved subsidizing Britain's competitors, Blair declared that any change in the budget must happen over time and respond to the 'legitimate needs of farming communities'.

This was to surrender most of the negotiating hand at the outset. Indeed the sole consequence of being willing to make concessions on such a scale over the CAP, and of pressing for investment in science and technology, was an implicit acceptance that the financial burden posed by the EU would increase. Already, with the rebate, Britain was providing a net contribution of £2.5 billion in 2003; and, without it, £5.95 billion. A cynic might refer to this as Blair's revenge on Brown, but the emphasis might just as much be on Blair's naïvety, his desire for popularity, or, indeed, the difficult situation in which Britain finds itself. In order to even propose modernization it is necessary to accept that the satisfaction of special interests, that is key to the CAP, must continue.

Furthermore, the increase in the number of member states ensures a greater problem with CAP reform as they expect their agricultural interests to be satisfied. The anger of the new member states about the delay in the budget deal reflects a challenge for the future, as there are now more interests to be satisfied. Poland has a particularly large farming sector, and Turkey has an even higher percentage of its population in farming. In 2004, the EU Commission estimated that Turkish agriculture would receive an annual subsidy of £5.5 billion.

A measure of scepticism is also offered by a historian's recourse to the previous time when the British held the presidency of the EU, in the first six months of 1998. Blair then offered a prospectus of reform, one in which Britain played a central role. He declared, significantly in a foreign city, The Hague, in January 1998, 'I am an optimist about Europe's future. For the path of reform and modernization is not just something peculiarly British but part of a movement for change in Europe.' Thus, 'a modern Britain in a modern Europe' was possible. Blair also identified the CAP as a key challenge, the point he made anew in 2005. At The Hague, he proclaimed the CAP 'a manifest absurdity' and declared: 'It is time to grasp fully the nettle of reform.' This was part of 'the new European consensus' that he saw emerging. This consensus entailed 'macro-economic stability…competition, liberalization and open markets' and 'active labour market policies', not state subsidies, over-regulation, welfare dependence and the unnecessary expansion of the public sector.

From the perspective of 2005, it is clear that very little was achieved. If CAP reform began in 2002, it is too little and too slow. More seriously, for expenditure on agriculture is an increasingly, but still very expensive and distorting, irrelevant distraction in a global trading system in which Brazil can meet many of Europe's needs, the burden on industry remains high, particularly in the shape of social welfare costs for labour, and it is unclear that large sections of the European economies can translate successfully to 'post-industrial' options. This reflects the failure of the aspirations agreed at the Lisbon Summit of 2000, in which the EU agreed that by 2010 it would be the most competitive, dynamic and knowledge-based economy in the world, as if that declaration would ensure these results. In the second quarter of 2005, GDP in the Euro area grew at an annual rate of 1.9 per cent (including the Netherlands at 4.9, Spain at 3.6, Italy at 2.8, France at 1.4, Belgium at 1.2 and Germany at nil) compared to 4.9 in Japan, 3.4 in the USA and 1.5 in Britain. Unemployment rates are difficult to compare but the comparable Euro area percentage figure was 8.9, compared to 5.5 for the USA, 4.8 for Britain and 4.6 for Japan. Within the Euro area, the Belgian rate was 12.8, the Spanish 11.1, the German 10.6, the French 10.0 and the Dutch 6.4. In Europe, however, there is a pronounced tendency to massage the figures, not least by the widespread registration of the unemployed as unable to work for health reasons. Heavily-subsidized higher education also cosmetically reduces unemployment. Irrespective of this, the very different growth rates for the Eurozone economies underlines the problems posed by the lack of exchange rate flexibility.

Alongside general burdens on EU manufacturing, it is worth noting the specific problems created for Britain by the continuation of Continental protectionism in trade in services, a protectionism that owes much to French policy. While British exports of services have been restricted, British agriculture, industry and finances have been hit by heavy imports of food and manufactured goods.[3]

One approach is to argue that the last few years have been taken up with important structural developments, in the shape of the Euro and enlargement, and that it is now time, after the failure of the project for a new constitution agreed, under French pressure, at the European summit at Nice in 2001, to return anew to a more reasonably modest pattern of development. This pattern is associated with the shift in the Presidency of the European Commission from Romano Prodi, a keen legislator who did not really work with the member states, to José Manuel Barroso, who is more cautious in backing EU legislation, and who wishes to work with the states, including Britain. In this context, the failure of Chirac and Schröder to push through their choice, Guy Verhofstadt, the Belgian Prime Minister, was of particular importance, as he is a keen integrationist, hostile to British assumptions, particularly economic reforms and co-operation with the USA. Instead, Blair and Berlusconi were instrumental in the choice of Barroso. An interpretation that places confidence in prospects for modest development and non-integrationism can see Britain as playing a major role, possibly indeed leading to a Blair Presidency of the European Commission.

This is a comforting proposition, but one that neglects the extent to which the French referendum was a vote against change. There is no reason to imagine that the French will accept major modifications to the CAP, and, indeed, in March 2005 Chirac forced the Commission to back down over its plan to open the EU's market in services. This Services Directive was important not only to the five-year 'jobs and growth' strategy for his Commission set out by Barroso in February 2005, but also for the prospect of British benefits from EU membership. If the French position offers a prospect of the isolation of France within the EU, that might serve to exert pressure on France, but such isolation is highly unlikely, not least because a CDU-SPD administration would wish to retain close Franco-German relations at the same time as improving those with Britain and the USA; while France is confident of the backing of Belgium and Luxembourg. Instead, the issues seen as comprising reform, principally the budget, treaty reform and enlargement, will all involve overlapping and shifting alliances that will make both success and failure less likely. Thus, we are back to the world of the fudge.

Furthermore, there are serious hostages to fortune in the approach adopted by Blair. Advocating a common foreign policy and shared defence capabilities makes scant sense in light of the determination of states to maintain their own voice, a position clearly taken by Britain, Italy, Poland, and Spain, as much as Belgium, France and Germany, in the debate over policy toward Iraq in 2003. More generally, the European 'project' is still being pushed by the Commission, with an attempt to implement quietly sections of the constitution even though they compromise national voices and perspectives. This is readily apparent with the preparations for an EU diplomatic system.

Another hostage to fortune is presented by the argument that the EU is out of touch. This is not a new claim. In April 1998, Blair wrote in the *Independent*, 'We have to explain and justify our vision. Our people will accept or rebel against it depending on how and where we move closer – and how well we as politicians explain our vision.' The extent to which confidence in the process of explanation is justified is unclear. While there is no alternative in a democracy, there is at times a naïve confidence that appropriate explanation will bring support and achieve consensus. This flies in the face of the need to achieve such consensus at both national and European levels, and the extent to which, at every level, European democracy is a matter of coalitions of votes with, in addition, scant willingness on the part of the unsuccessful to accept unwelcome verdicts. Correspondingly, in the governmental sphere, there is a mixture of inter-governmentalism and supranationalism, and the essentially complex and unfixed nature of this process always makes consensus elusive.

If Blair's position is difficult, that of the other two major British political parties is also troublesome. The Liberal Democrats' practice of promising all things to all voters, and of trying to create broad constituencies of support, faces difficulties when the focus moves from neighbourhood politics, which is their forte, to matters of national or international importance. These issues threaten to accentuate the contrasts between what the party appears to stand for, and thus to oppose, in different parts of the country. For example, the Liberal Democrats in Scotland, Wales and south-east England find it easier, and more necessary, to strike a Euro-enthusiastic note than their counterparts in the West Country, an area of traditional and growing Liberal strength that has suffered heavily from membership of the EU. This is particularly the case with the fishing and agriculture of the region. Although their share of the economy of the West Country is declining, they are still important in its identity, particularly fishing for Cornwall. Nevertheless, the skill the Liberal Democrats have shown in avoiding firm commitments and their ability to play the anti-politics card is notable and likely to save them from the contradictions of their position over the EU. The Tories have been less adroit tactically.

The Tories are in a far less fortunate position, in large part because of the legacy of their divisions over the issue. This has helped make the EU a potent issue in the identification of internal differences and in the pursuit of political advantage. Furthermore, the totemic nature of the issue took precedence over that of modernization in terms of the debates over the Tory future in the 1990s and early 2000s, helping ensure that the party did not have a future in the short-term. Moreover, Europe as an issue opened up divisions between the Parliamentary Party and the Party in the country, helping, in particular, to sow distrust over the former among the latter. Part of the legacy was the Iain Duncan Smith leadership of 2001-3, one that was unfortunate in terms of addressing the need to win over much of the electorate. Historical revisionism frequently goes to great lengths, but it is difficult to see Duncan Smith being treated in the future as a great Party leader, let alone a Prime Minister alas *manqué*. Although a Maastricht rebel, and clearly not Kenneth Clarke, he was unable anyway to offer a robust line on the EU. In 2003, in his speech 'A New Europe of Democracies', delivered in Prague, Duncan Smith declared: 'The Conservative Party's commitment to the European Union is rooted in our commitment to the permanent interests and values of the British people', a contradiction in terms to many of the voters the Conservatives needed to rally.

Conservative divisions over Europe are not only a matter of opportunities lost, but also one of problems for the future. This appears demonstrated by the psephology of recent elections. The creation of single-issue, anti-EU parties – the Referendum Party, UK Independence Party and Veritas – seriously weakened the Conservatives by cutting their vote, but also reflected popular support for a Euro-sceptic voice. It would be misleading to suggest that everyone who voted for these parties would otherwise have voted Conservative, for the Euro-sceptic camp includes many non-Conservatives. Yet, former Conservatives are represented disproportionately among these fringe parties. In 1999, UKIP gained 7 per cent of the vote and won three seats in the Euro-elections, a credible result for a new party; in 2001 it polled 1.47 per cent of the vote in the general election; in 2004 16 per cent in the European elections and won twelve seats; and, in 2005, despite a public split shortly before the election that led to the departure of Robert Kilroy-Silk to form Veritas, 2.38 per cent in the general election. That does not sound very much, but the margin between Labour and Conservatives in 2005 was a narrow one (35.2 per cent to 32.3 per cent). If added to the Conservatives, the votes cast for UKIP and Veritas would have made the percentage figures very different. In terms of constituency results, the over-representation of Labour would have limited the consequences, but, nevertheless, the Conservatives would have won 27 constituencies but for UKIP and Veritas votes, and this would have cut the Labour majority to 49.

This indicates the extent to which an explicit Euro-scepticism on the part of the Conservatives might well help the Party electorally, whatever the pressure from members of the Party against such an option. In the 2005 election, the Conservatives were opposed to the Euro and the constitution and supported the repeal of the social chapter, the repatriation of fisheries and foreign aid to the national level, and the repeal, in part, of the European Convention on Human Rights; but the Party made little of Europe. Talk of flexibility did not engage the public. This was probably a serious tactical mistake in electoral terms, even if it helped the Conservatives avoid public disputes over the issue during the campaign, both within the Party and in response to external scrutiny.

It would have been more appropriate to admit past mistakes, particularly at Maastricht, and suggest present remedies. One aspect of the mistake was that by failing to emphasize the European issue, the Conservatives passed up an opportunity to emphasize the difference between the political Parties. This was not least in terms of the possibility of creating blue water between their stance and that of both the Liberals and Labour and then using this to lump the latter two together and to suggest that support for one was akin to backing for the other. This was serious as there are signs that this difference was what much of the electorate wanted. This was comparable to the Conservative failure to engage seriously over tax cutting.

The Conservative Party has the opportunity of offering leadership in both these respects, capturing popular discontent, and shaping it in accordance of Conservative goals of national and personal liberty, goals that cut across social divisions and inherited perceptions of political identities. Indeed, tax and Europe can be joined as issues by pointing out the dangers posed by EU pressure for tax harmonization. EU commissioners allege that different tax rates pose the risk of unfair competition and also harm EU revenues. The pressure for harmonization affects all EU states, whether or not they are part of the Eurozone. If the Conservatives fail to take the opportunity, they may be outflanked, not only by UKIP, but, more seriously, by Labour if, under a Brown leadership, it adopts a robust, nationalist position different to that of Blair. The latter prospect poses a particular challenge for the Conservatives. There may indeed be a repetition, albeit in a different form, of the response among some to the first Blair government. Relief that he distanced himself from the left and continued some of the Conservatives' policies led to a failure to devote sufficient attention to the dangerous attitudes, initiatives and practices of the government.

There may be a similarly mistaken response to a Brown government. The ABT approach, 'Anyone but Tony', may lead to Brown being given too soft a ride. In some circles, this may be taken further by a disengagement from Iraq, while Eurosceptics are likely to applaud, if only from relief, any signs of a firmer approach towards the EU. However, there is a need for considerable caution about Brown's assumptions concerning Britain's role within the EU. There is the danger that Brown pushes the country in a leftward direction and then uses membership of the corporationist EU to entrench his policies, thus thwarting, or limiting, the prospect of any reversal of policy at the national level. This was part of a pattern in British relations within the EU. In the 1970s, the Heathite Conservatives sought to entrench a market-oriented, mixed economy by means of British membership in the EU. Similarly, in the late 1980s, the left sought to entrench what they saw as social rights, including the dominant position of trade unions, away from the pressure of domestic politics in terms of the Thatcher government. Even if Brown seeks to maintain national autonomy (sovereignty has long since gone), there is the danger that he himself, and/or his Labour colleagues and successors, will temper this in order to entrench their vision of social justice. In practical terms, the EU vista of using political assertion as an attempt to negate economic reality and the freedom of individual producers and consumers, matches the thrust of traditional Labour suppositions.

Assumptions about the situation in a Brown premiership do not free the Conservatives from the need to address the issue, and the retirement or death of prominent Europhiles, such as Heseltine and Heath, have made this a less divisive option, although, in 2005, it affected discussion about Kenneth Clarke as a potential leader. As part of confronting the issue of national identity, the Conservatives also need to revisit the question of Britishness and the constitutional relations between the parts of the United Kingdom. This is not incompatible with the idea of recovering an English identity, particularly in order to define an alternative to the support from Labour and the EU (via the EU Committee of the

Regions) for regional assemblies. An English constitutional identity would provide a representation that could compete with those of Scotland and Wales in order to give due weight to English interests within both Britain and the EU. By English, it is of course understood that the definition is in terms of the inhabitants of England, not an ethnic group.

On the British scale, the Conservatives need to address the consequences of the weakening in recent decades of what had been traditional, and still vital, benchmarks of national identity: parliamentary sovereignty, national independence, the Common Law, the monarchy, the Church of England and a culture tolerance. Furthermore, the Conservatives have to consider their response to the failure to create viable alternatives to these benchmarks. Labour offered a supposed set of modish national values, some of which looked back to pragmatic, liberal, puritan and utilitarian accounts of identity and history that had developed on the left, but most of which, instead, were based on modish urban life. These were the politics of Blair and Peter Mandelson, but they proved unacceptable to many Labour politicians. Tessa Jowell, Secretary of State for Culture, Media and Sport, stated in November 2001, 'You can't distil our national character to a liking for designer water or retro lamps.'

As a result of its modishness, New Labour was less able to elicit sustained popular support, let alone enthusiasm, than the essentially apolitical and value-weak interlocked cultures of sport, television and celebrity. Blair sought to reach out to these cultures, but his ability to make his policies attractive to this world proved short-lived as well as superficial. The Conservatives, however, have largely failed to engage with these cultures, and, if this has spared them a demeaning modishness of scant lasting value, it is also an aspect of their limited popular support.

At the same time, if its policies towards the EU are more clear-cut, the Conservative Party will face criticism not only on the head of Euro-scepticism but, more specifically, on that of tactics. In particular, it will be argued that any Conservative policy involving renegotiation is extremist as it represents withdrawal, that this is against the national interest, and that the very danger that such a perception will be widespread will lead to the Conservatives losing support. On the other hand, to press for reform without retaining the option for departure to join, for example, Norway, Iceland and Lichtenstein in the European Economic Area, or to have bilateral agreements with the EU as Switzerland does, would gravely weaken Britain's negotiating hand. It would also serve to remind the public about the repeated drift of British policy and the way in which promises that further concessions would not be made have generally proved fruitless. Furthermore, reform short of renegotiation is not credible, no more than policy negotiation without the option of the veto; and renegotiation includes the option of admitting failure. Renegotiation is essentially an intergovernmental strategy, and not an integrationist one. Indeed, since recovering and being willing to use, the national veto should be a key objective for countries (not just Britain) worried about integrationism; it is best to face the logic of this policy. The Conservatives also need to accept that they will always be stigmatized by their opponents as extremist. They should not allow fear of this charge to set their agenda. The charge is untrue in itself, and has not prevented about a third of the voters from supporting the Party. There is scant sign that more will rally if the extremist label is not applied, and there is no reason to believe that such a slandering will not happen whatever the Conservative purpose.

1 A. Cowgill, *The European Constitution in Perspective: Analysis and Review of The Treaty Establishing A Constitution for Europe* (London, 2004); S. Sexton, *A Guide to the Treaty Establishing a European Constitution* (London, 2005).
2 D. Dinar, *Europe Recast: A History of the European Union* (Basingstoke, 2004).
3 P. Minford, V. Mahambare and E. Nowell, *Should Britain Leave the EU? An Economic Analysis of a Troubled Relationship* (Cheltenham, 2005).

CHAPTER 7

CONCLUSIONS: CRISIS OF A POLITICAL SYSTEM?

Problems in British relations with the EU are powerfully linked to the issue of democratic deficit stemming from the view that Brussels lacks accountability and fairness, an opinion also expressed about British elections, not least after that of 2005. There was also a subtext arising from relations within the UK, specifically concern within Scotland and Wales about the nature of representation within Britain. Far from these issues being largely a matter of political techniques and tactics, there was a serious problem of viability. A political system cannot work unless the bulk of the population feels some sense of identity. Related to, and, in part, due to the EU, this sense is now weakening, at the same time that patterns of deference encouraging consent are also eroding. The British, indeed, are becoming more ungovernable.

Yet, at the same time, the EU has failed to replace the nation as a focus for popular identity, and thus loyalty. If this is a measure of its failure, it is also a cause of it. The central political problem in any community is the eliciting of consent. This is not simply a question of defining acceptable policies, and of selecting leaders who will be judged competent, but also reflects the nature of identification between people and government, which is a question of history, symbolism, and a sense of place and purpose. These, in turn, combine to produce an ideology that is more potent than the more intellectual and abstract creeds designated by that term. Despite all the talk of the failure and redundancy of the nation-state, and the need for replacing it by power-sharing, supranational bodies and Euroregions, the last outlined in the Maastricht Treaty, it is the nation-state that is most effective at eliciting and securing consent.

It is no accident, indeed, that Euro-federalism is endorsed most strongly by peoples whose nation-states are recent and weak (in face of regional and other divisions), namely Belgium and Italy. However, this is not the case with all recent nation-states. In the Czech Republic in July 2005, Václav Kalus, the President, who saw the projected constitution as unconstitutional, pressed for the replacement of the EU by the Organisation of European States, a projected free-trade system. Earlier, 'A Europe of Democracies', the report of the minority Democracy Forum on the Convention of the Future of Europe which drew up the proposed constitution, had suggested a similar system based on self-governing countries, with the focus on national Parliaments. Their amendments during the convention were ignored, as was their report, and the British government did nothing to prevent this. Instead, Blair preferred horse-trading over the constitution with Giscard d'Estaing, who had treated the Democracy Forum with contempt.

In contrast to Belgium and Italy, Britain and Denmark see far less support for Euro-federalism, and France, another country with a strong sense of identity and interest, registered an important criticism in 2005. It is instructive to note that in Denmark there is a constitutional obligation for referenda on all international treaties. It would be a mistake to argue that all recently independent nation-states endorse Euro-federalism. This is not the case in Scandinavia where Norway rejected the EU, and Finland is not the keenest state for integration. Indeed, the recently independent states of Eastern Europe, while welcoming membership of the West through NATO, the EU and the Euro, may well display a determination to preserve their independence.

The problems, nevertheless, for many countries of one-state politics and the limitations of one-state solutions encourage the search for solutions at the EU level. This was seen in Germany in the early 2000s, as both electorate and politicians found it difficult to face up to the need to keep the economy competitive and to look at the costs of social welfare. In September 2002, the German electorate re-elected the Social

Democrat and Green coalition, the less radical choice. This government then acted like a small version of the EU, with political division and unpopularity greeting the attempts to reform the economy, not least in order to provide the growth necessary to help the 4.7 million unemployed. The government's Agenda 2010 economic reform programme was rejected by left-wing critics within the government, and the Social Democrats lost control of North-Rhine Westphalia, its key electoral stronghold and Germany's most populous province. On 1 July 2005, Schröder deliberately triggered a parliamentary vote of no confidence in order to prepare the way for a general election a year early.

Schröder's speech in the Bundestag spoke more generally to the political failure not only of Germany, but also of the Stability and Growth Pact and the EU:

> 'The steady confidence that I need to carry out my reforms is no longer present even within my own coalition government. Dissent and criticism of my policies are on the increase. This is a high price to pay for reform.'

In practice, the reforms offered in both Germany and the EU were top-down, putting government first and leaving the individual only limited competences. That was a measure of both the character and the failure of the political system: the automatic assumption was that of direction by those who knew best.

If German difficulties can be related to those of the EU, the problems of Italian politics are also indicative. Charges brought against recent leaders such as Andreotti, Craxi and the current Prime Minister, Silvio Berlusconi, are suggestive of a political culture mired in self-interest and institutionalized corruption. The willingness to change the law in order to help Berlusconi avoid trial on false accounting charges is not too dissimilar to the EU's willingness to cover up serious fraud in both the Commission and the Eurostat. Whistleblowers have been disciplined (could that ever happen in Blair's Britain?), while police raids have been mounted to seize the confidential files of investigative journalists.

It is also possible to exaggerate the effectiveness of the nation-state as a representative political unit. There is a kind of circularity: the nation-state represents national interest effectively because its very existence defines these interests. What is less clear is that the interests thus defined and pursued by the nation-state are the primary interests of the people of that state. Nevertheless, given that these interests do not exist clearly, except in the most basic terms, outside the political process, the nation-state plays a crucial role in discussing, defining and validating such interests. It is far from clear that a European political community can successfully fulfil the same function, certainly in terms of obtaining popular support.

This owes much to the role of historical formation in giving identities and meaning to the lives of political communities. Yet, the recent history of much of Continental Europe was so unwelcome that it is scarcely surprising that the bout of new constitutionalism that followed 1945 made scant attempt to look for roots or continuities. Within this context, the creation of the EEC (as a way to root democracies at the national level, although not democracy at the European level) appeared sensible, and its norms seemed appropriate, just as the response in Britain was understandably different. The EEC was a reaction not only to recent, but also to earlier European history. In place of the national-cum-ideological hegemony sought by the French Revolutionaries and Hitler, and the national dominance pursued by Napoleon and Wilhelm II of Germany, there was a resolute attempt to create a supranational system that sought both to supersede national interests and to create a structure of national and institutional power-sharing.

At least initially the EEC can be seen as a defence mechanism for vulnerable nation-states. This is in part a question of the specific goals of particular states in the mid-1950s, and in light of the argument that international organizations are set up by nations in order to protect themselves and their sovereignty from growing economic and political interdependence. From this perspective, the British did not share the interests of other states in joining a body such as this. If the EEC is seen as having been generated by particular interpretations of national interest, then attention has to be focused on the fears and aspirations of the late 1940s and 1950s, and on the diplomacy of those years. France wanted the ECSC and the EEC to help modernization, but also to control Germany, and she wished to control German independence so much that it was worth some loss of sovereignty to achieve this vital national aim; a national interest which the British did not share to the same extent. Germany and Italy wanted the EEC to safeguard their democracies, again a need Britain did not share, but one later shared by Spain, Greece and Eastern Europe. Despite the arguments of the enthusiastic federalists of the period, few of the Continental leaders of the 1950s saw the EEC as likely to replace the nation-states, but, in a Europe suffering from devastation, political dislocation and international division stemming from the traumatic events of the 1940s, the EEC offered a means to create space for development.

Britain, in turn, only sought to join when the EEC became an apparent threat to her in terms of growing economic competitiveness and international relevance, and the same might be argued of the ERM. In this light, recent British alienation and distance from Euro-convergence is unsurprising. It has, indeed, become far stronger as the limited objectives of most of the politicians who constructed the EEC developed in more ambitious directions, which created a different political threat for British governments. This threat was not simply viewed in the light of misplaced fears, populism or even xenophobia.

Unlike African and Asian international bodies, all the members of the EU are, of course, democracies, and the institutions of the EU are thus filled, directly or indirectly, as a consequence of democratic processes, or at least ostensibly democratic processes. Comparisons between the EU and the former Soviet Union[1] are, at least at present, far fetched. Yet, focusing on the difficulties confronting the attempt to create a plausible European public myth helps to explain some of the problems faced by any attempt to displace the nation-state from its position in popular loyalties. A sense of place and continuity is crucial to the harmony of individuals and societies, and this affects the response to the currents of change that have become so insistent over the last century. In particular, the notion of a European state and/or nation lacks roots, and the impact of the very different roots of other political and ethnic groups make it unlikely that a new identity can be successfully created.

At this crucial level, the notion of European community is of value only if its institutional pretensions and prerogatives do not range too widely, and are restricted by the preservation of a major role for the nation-state. Telling people and their elected representatives that, as they are Europeans, they must act, indeed think, in a certain fashion is unacceptable in a democratic society, particularly as it is employed to deny the validity of their sense of identity and the views that arise from it. A key aspect of free choice is that people should be able to choose the level at which they wish to express and make their free choice, and this was at stake in referenda about the Euro and the European constitution. To argue that they are wrong on functional or practical grounds is inherently undemocratic. Political goals should derive from the identities and interests of individuals freely expressed. They are not fixed and, instead, are subject to the changes that are naturally a product of the use of free will.

If, therefore, the exercise of free will leads to an integrationist European Union, the organization and goals of the latter should be such that they can adapt to the withdrawal of support or a major change in direction. There is no sign that the EU, as currently conceived, possesses those characteristics or seeks those competences. Indeed, not only its structures and processes, but also the convictions of its supporters, make the EU singularly unable to respond not only to popular opinion but also to changing circumstances. For ideological and functional reasons, it is easy to understand that those who see government as a response process find it easiest to conceive of this at the national level. This also best allows for the nature of change not as a linear, uni-directional and predictable process, as conceived of by those who support the European 'project', but as variable, unpredictable and experienced in a very diverse fashion.

CONCLUSIONS

In defending the configuration and continuity of British practices, politicians are fighting not for selfish national interests, but for the sense of the living past that is such a vital component of a people's understanding, acceptance and appreciation of their own society and identity. This sense of a living past, and of the loyalties and identities bound up in it, seems to mean little either to Blair, with his conviction about the value of the future, or to those who press the case for a European identity for Britain. Their policies should be rejected not only because they are inappropriate for Britain and, indeed, the other members of the EU, but also because the assumptions that underlie and motivate them are misconceived and dangerous.

1   V. Bukovsky and P. Stroilov, *EUSSR: The Soviet Roots of European Integration* (London, 2005).